'Julia Pascal's *Honeypot* is the most astoun[c]
writing I've seen th[..]
Jonathan Watson, *The Stage*

'It is a fascinating glimpse of a world one knows exists but is rarely reported. This isn't a play that takes sides – it is indicting both of them.'
Howard Loxton, *British Theatre Guide*

'The relationships between the characters were intriguing and there was not a moment that I was not engaged.'
Louise Franks, *The Public Reviews*

'Where *Honeypot* works terrifically well is with the state of mind of the warring Semites. When Koby tells the blonde Susanne that she is "what every Arab and Jewish man wants", there is something in that generalisation that reveals the mores of the men fighting the Middle-East war.'
John Nathan, *The Jewish Chronicle*.

'I'm moved and haunted by *Nineveh*.
One can't pay a play a greater compliment'
Lady Antonia Fraser.

'Julia Pascal's script draws on myth and magic realism, and there are shades of both Sartre's *Huis Clos* and *Waiting for Godot* as the men try to make sense of their situation. At times it feels as if we are not just inside the whale's belly, but in the nightmarish landscapes of the men's minds as they try to suppress the memories of their acts of murder, rape and mutilation. It takes the arrival of a child with a sewn-up mouth to help them find a way to speak the truth.'
Lyn Gardner, *The Guardian*

'Pascal's comic touch and the cast's fearless performances combine to hold our attention.'
Honour Bayes, *Time Out*

'…an ambitious script – where not a word is wasted – by Julia Pascal. *Nineveh*'s story is universal, just like the story of Jonah and the whale.'
Lauren Paxman, *The Stage*

'This play seemed to have been written by a male writer as all the dialogue between soldiers sounds true: harsh and brutal at times and also romantically naïve. We (in the USSR) were brought up with this grand idea of children's heroism which my country experienced during WW2 but this play clearly showed me that it is a tragedy not a heroic act when a child is involved in a war.'
Katerina Linnik (Arkharova), *BBC Russian Service*

JULIA PASCAL
POLITICAL PLAYS

Honeypot

Broken English

Nineveh

Woman On The Bridge

OBERON BOOKS
LONDON

WWW.OBERONBOOKS.COM

First published in 2013 by Oberon Books Ltd
521 Caledonian Road, London N7 9RH
Tel: +44 (0) 20 7607 3637 / Fax: +44 (0) 20 7607 3629
e-mail: info@oberonbooks.com
www.oberonbooks.com

A catalogue record for this book is available from the British
Library.

PB ISBN: 978-1-78319-038-6
E ISBN: 978-1-78319-537-4

Cover design by James Illman

Printed and bound by Marston Book Services, Didcot.

Visit www.oberonbooks.com to read more about all our books
and to buy them. You will also find features, author interviews and
news of any author events, and you can sign up for e-newsletters
so that you're always first to hear about our new releases.

In loving memory of my aunt, Edith Newman.
Our political discussions still remain in my mind.

Contents

Preface   9

Honeypot   17

Broken English   83

Nineveh   147

Woman On The Bridge   195

Preface

Writing a play has always been a political act for me. *Far Above Rubies*, my first production looked critically at the effect of Islam and Judaism on women's lives. *Theresa* revealed the hidden history of British collaboration with the Nazis in the Channel Islands. *Year Zero* was set in Vichy-occupied France. *St Joan* was an attack on French racism. The action in *Crossing Jerusalem* is set during the suicide bombings of the 2002 intifada. *The Shylock Play* viewed *The Merchant of Venice* through the eyes of a Warsaw Ghetto survivor. The larger canvas of world politics and the smaller battlefield of family wars fuel many of my texts. The connection between the two is not a mistake.

The family and its breakdown is the starting point of *Honeypot* which was inspired by interviews I had in Israel with a former Mossad agent, a Christian Swede I call Susanne. She had worked for Mossad as a honeypot and her job was to seduce and kill the enemy of the state. This entailed travelling to Paris and other major European cities to encounter the men she was to assassinate. Hers was an extraordinary story.

Of course much of the action in *Honeypot* is imagined. As with the characters of Esther in *The Yiddish Queen Lear*, and Varda in *Crossing Jerusalem*, I wanted to write a woman who would be considered 'a bad mother.' Susanne leaves her baby daughter and failing marriage to commit murder. I invented a backstory for the play which would give Susanne a reason for such a mission. It had to be an emotional one that was to become political. When she discovers her father's hidden Jewish identity this awakens something inside her. Even though he is dead she is still seeking his approval. She wants to 'do something Jewish', to connect with him and his past. It is this which mobilises her to volunteer as a honeypot.

This was not quite enough though to send her on such a dangerous mission. I had to invent Susanne's fractured marriage and her promiscuity so that she would be independent and without any emotional anchor. Her amorality, a trait which would be criticised in 'normal' society, is a key asset in her career as a spy. As a traditional Scandinavian blonde, she does not use her looks as a narcissist might. They are merely useful as a political weapon. Susanne is no stereotype of dumb blonde, she is smart, manipulative and vulnerable. Her journey from being a wife and mother in name only, to a woman who finally learns to love her girl, is the arc in the play.

Creating a character who commits such a provocative act was also a political act for me as a writer because, on the English stage, it is rare to see a female protagonist engaged in politics. I wanted to challenge the status quo by creating a complex woman who is aware of the dangerous political world she infiltrates.

Honeypot was produced just before the 2012 London Games to remind us of what happened in the 1972 Munich Olympics. The roles of Koby, the Mossad trainer and Joseph, the former PLO activist, were written to be played by one actor, as a way of challenging any possible Jewish or Arab stereotyping. My text was also a small way of honouring the lives of the eleven murdered Israeli athletes. At the opening of the London Olympics, the Committee refused any public acknowledgment of this horrifying murder of Jews on German soil.

The styles of each play in this volume are different and range from naturalism to absurdism. But there are thematic links. All explore the im/morality of murder.

Broken English opens up a difficult political territory for British Jews and perhaps many would rather forget this particular history. In 1946 there was a plot by Jewish nationalists to assassinate the British Foreign Secretary, Ernest Bevin. It was he who was considered responsible for the limitation of Jewish entry into British Mandate Palestine after the Holocaust. Political action was planned to focus public opinion on the plight of concentration camp victims who wanted to resettle in Palestine. This forgotten British-Jewish history raises questions around identity, violence and allegiance to the homeland.

The action takes place in one room. Harry's flat. I wanted to set it in the East End where Jewish Communists and Socialists had fought with Oswald Mosley's Fascists in the 1930s. The construction of the character of Harry, is as a result of meetings with two different men. One, and I shall call him Mr X, had been part of the original cell destined to carry out this murder. When I met this elderly man, he was secretive about me revealing his name or the names of others in his group. However he did say that Menachim Begin had planned to come to England as leader of this action which was, of course, aborted. Why? Was Begin stopped at the docks? Since meeting Mr X, The National Archives in Kew have endorsed this conversation as did *Document*, a BBC Radio documentary, broadcast in 2007. This revealed how a few women, mainly living in Golders Green, were also involved. They too did not wish to reveal their names but admitted hiding guns to be smuggled to Palestine.

The second man who contributed to the character of Harry was Mr Y. I met him at a Passover dinner in a west London suburb. He revealed how an adulterous relationship with a neighbour twenty five years earlier, had resulted in a son. His lover had passed this child off as her husband's. Now that she was widowed she felt Mr Y should know the truth. At this meal he was nervously talking to me about an imminent meeting with his newly found son. His secret prompted me to write about the pride a man might feel discovering a new son but also about his feelings of rivalry. The young man reminds him of his own ageing process. A son's virility can threaten a father's diminishing sexual power. In *The Yiddish Queen Lear* and *Crossing Jerusalem*, the tension between mothers and daughters was a recurring theme which grew from observations about my mother and her sisters. While writing *Broken English*, it seemed natural to chart the rivalry between between fathers and sons. Here the role of Joseph was inspired by many of the Irish Jews in my father's family. Few are aware of the importance of Irish Jewish history unless they have read James Joyce's *Ulysses* and have encountered Leopold Bloom. When I read Bloom's voice it reminds me of my father's. The mixture of Irish and Yiddish speech rhythms that are Joseph's reveal an immigrant experience that doubly reflects a particular historical moment: the Jewish and Irish desire for nationhood. As an Irishman and a Jew, Joseph's Zionism is informed by Irish nationalism. His character, however is conflicted. He is both the Jew who refuses to kill his enemy and the Jew who must.

There were others who helped me understand the atmosphere and history of 1945-1948. Alain Franck the French writer and translator, remembered French Socialists, Gaullists and Communists helping Jews smuggle arms to Palestine. When I asked him why such a diversity of groups had supported Jewish nationalism, he replied, 'because they hated the British'! The Hungarian Holocaust survivor, and later the Israeli Embassy London Cultural Attaché, Kariel Gardosh, spoke to me about being imprisoned in Acre jail for drawing anti-British cartoons. These testimonies helped me build the climate of those terrible years for Jews. Between 1945-1948, the majority no longer felt safe in the cemetery of Europe but, even though many wished for a homeland in Israel, they also knew that a Jewish nation state would provoke geopolitical problems. *Broken English* is set just after the blowing up of the King David Hotel in 1946 when British Jews were in a moral dilemma. The pro and anti-Zionist debate of postwar Europe still divides and has resonances for many other communities.

Woman On The Bridge was born from discovering how many women in my own family were suicides. The silence and shame around these deaths provoked me to research women's self destructive behaviour by reading psychiatric studies. After interviews between 2009 and 2012 with the psychotherapist Patricia Polledri, I became aware of inherited trauma and how it is transmitted across generations. *Ghosts From The Nursery* by Robin Karr-Morse and Meredith S. Wiley (Grove Atlantic,1997) was my primary research. Through this, and wider reading, my aim was to create a new character in British drama: that of the non-hysterical suicidal Jewish woman.

Judith, is a fifty-five-year-old London radio journalist, whose marriage is cracking. Her flight to Manhattan, and the people she meets there, awaken a cycle of masked depression that was seeded in babyhood. Judith's journey to the Bridge, and her impulse to jump off it, is motivated by the subconscious. On her Ulyssian journey she is also carrying the absent dead. She discovers her trauma through her relationships with Andy her one night stand, Anna her 110-year-old great aunt, Louise the East European Jewish survivor, Susan the drug addict but, most importantly, through her meeting with Gloria, a Catholic Puerto Rican New York cop whose mission is to avenge dead women.

Writing this play forced me to consider how to show inner-destructive impulses without exposition or leading the character to the psychiatrist's couch. This text follows the structure of David Mamet's drama, *Edmond*, where a man goes on a journey and is changed by those he meets. This crazy voyage is also one I love in Ibsen's *Peer Gynt*. Unlike Mamet and Ibsen, I wanted my 'Ulysses' to be a female character. Judith starts the play already carrying the weight of a family history in her unconscious. How could I reveal this, and her mental breakdown, subtly? In a reading held at New York University's London campus before The League of Professional Theatre Women in 2012, one audience member was surprised when Judith got up onto the ledge of Brooklyn Bridge. Her reaction was, 'Judith doesn't seem mad' which pleased me. Newspaper reports often note how a suicide's friends are, 'shocked at this uncharacteristic behaviour'.

As Dr Andrew Crowcroft notes, in *The Psychotic. Understanding Madness* (Penguin Books 1968). 'There is a condition called a smiling depression. The patient may be severely depressed and yet in an interview his features are mobile and he can even smile. It is when he has a silent, inactive moment that he may become suddenly *en rapport* with himself and become aware of his despair'.

Such silent moments are plotted into the stage directions. Judith beats a chair violently or moves towards the subway platform edge as the train arrives. The compulsion to disappear is a visual one here.

Of course it is Judith's clash with the life-affirming Gloria that pushes her to change. The creation of Gloria was inspired by interviews with the retired New York cop, Irma Duffy, whose generosity allowed me to construct a character that has emerged from our many discussions.

Nineveh was the result of a meeting with the American director Ailin Conant who commissioned the text for her company Theatre Témoin. She had been leading The Return Project which entailed her travelling to Israel, Kashmir Lebanon and Rwanda to interview middle-aged former fighters or young boy soldiers. Some of these were suffering from post-traumatic stress syndrome. Conant gave me a collection of testimonies where no clear narrative line emerged. What did hit me though was that all the murders were spoken of within a moral framework. The men, most of whom were in their forties, seemed to be asking how could they live with what they had done? Was guilt ever to disappear? How can a man forgive himself and how can he repair?

The question now centred around feelings of shame and sin. From Rwanda Conant brought the story of a boy being swallowed by a fish. Clearly this was a version of *Jonah and the Whale* and a key to the dramaturgy. It pushed me to imagine these four fighters as four Jonahs. Stuck in the belly of a whale what might they discuss? What might they do? How can they get out? These questions drive the action. The concept of the whale also had an added bonus in a play without women. She was a womb where the men might grow and be re-birthed. This setting allowed me to create a mythical level; the men were in a limbo from which they might escape but would they crawl out of the whale into another war zone and, if so, would they again return to killing?

If the whale offered me an answer to where the narrative should be situated there was still another problem to be solved. I could find no cultural or political connections between Kashmir and Rwanda even if there was one between Israel and Lebanon. Therefore the next question to ask was who are these soldiers? My decision was not to give them specific national identities. They were Mr Everysoldier. And yet they could not be neutral. The answer was to construct four conflicting archetypes. Joel is The Joker but also partly L'Idiot Savant. Johnny is the Leader who loses his dominance. Richie is the Eternal Student and Chance is The Innocent-But-Corrupted Child. Each has a terrible history which would emerge in different ways but how could I show their post-traumatic stress? Perhaps they would not all talk about what they had done. Revelation would be determined by character and the dynamic of the group. This collective energy is also affected by the entrance of the silent child soldier, Chance. His character was enriched by meeting twenty-seven-year-old Sierra Leonian, Messeh Leone, who has worked with those affected by conflict in Africa. Leone told me stories remembered by children forced into war, and, through his ability to convey the village atmosphere, I was able to create Chance whose physicality was also influenced by another bloody history: Iran.

Sally Mijit, who teaches English to refugees and asylum seekers at Westminster Kingsway College, asked me if I would like to meet an Iranian dissident who had sewn his lips as a protest against deportation by the British government in 2011. He was Keyvan Bahari, one of four Iranian asylum seekers on hunger strike. These Iranian dissidents knew that a return to Iran would mean certain execution. Their action was featured in the British media and ultimately, the men were allowed to stay. When I met Bahari in 2013, I could still see the scars around his mouth where he had pushed in the needle and the cat gut. The image of sewn lips worked on my imagination in many ways. It meant that speaking was agony. Each of my characters was unable to easily talk of his murderous past. To suppress their atrocities, Johnny, Richie and Joel had metaphorically sewn their own lips. Therefore the image seemed both theatrical and psychologically authentic. By transposing the action of an Iranian refugee to the character of an African child soldier-victim, I felt I was able to show the internal and the external wounds.

Character construction is a mysterious journey and can be stimulated by fusing several experiences. Chance's story may have been African but it was also layered by these Iranian asylum-seekers in London. Yet Chance's voice had to be that of a young African boy not that of a sophisticated Persian-speaking intellectual. Encounters with my African neighbours and those I heard on London buses helped me find a voice for Chance. He must be an innocent child but also a killer. The character is both young and old. Leone gave me details about the African diamond wars and this knowledge allowed me to create Chance as a victim of mercenary armies who would cut open a man's stomach to search for hidden diamonds. Through such images I realised the dangerous power of this precious stone and how a diamond could be a leitmotif in the text.

A diamond symbolises love, marriage, the possibility of erotic happiness, everything that is missing in the lives of Joel,

Richie and Johnny but here it is also associated with theft, greed and murder. The diamond, like The Book that Richie clutches, brings the outer world into the belly of the whale. *Who is allowed to see what is in books?* is also a dramatic question between the glued pages that are finally torn open. The Book contains images from the liberation of Belsen and brings the voices of the dead onstage. This moment asks can a book transform a killer into a future president? When Chance kisses it, he does not know that he is mirroring the 5,000 year old act of Jews honouring their prayer book in the synagogue. It is the child who is able to suggest transformation through learning. He falls in love with The Book and this action ends the play with hope.

Julia Pascal, October 2013

HONEYPOT

Honeypot is dedicated to the memory of Martha Gellhorn.

Honeypot by Julia Pascal premiered on 11 October 2011
at the New Diorama Theatre

    Cast:
    SUSANNE   Jessica Claire
    KOBY/JOSEPH   Paul Herzberg

    Voices off:
    Phillip Arditti, Michael Borch, Amir Boutros, Patric Deony,
    Alain Carpentier, Ruth Posner, Orly Rabinyan, Robert Littos,
    Peter Silverleaf.

    Directed by Orly Rabinyan
    Designed by Claire Lyth
    Lighting by Jessica Faulks
    Sound design by Dan Hunt
    Graphic Design by Eugenie Dodd

A Brief History

Israel-Palestine in the twentieth century.

At the end of World War 1, the defeat of the Ottoman Empire meant the end of Muslim rule in the territory and the area was mandated by the British until 1948 when the State of Israel was formed.

Jews and Arabs had lived together under the Ottomans. However the prevailing mood of late nineteenth century nationalism encouraged Jews from Europe and Russia to dream of a Jewish state. (Zionism).

The idea of a country for Jews was strengthened by the Tsarist pogroms and by the rise in anti-semitism during the Hitler years (1933-1945). However the British mandate severely restricted Jewish entry to Palestine both before and after World War Two.

The state of Israel was declared in 1947 at the United Nations.

When Jews celebrated the birth of Israel in May 1948, Arab citizens recognised this as the beginning of The Catastrophe (Naqba).

In June 1967, (The Six Day War), Israel took over the West Bank, Gaza and the city of Jerusalem. This occupation is still at the heart of today's political controversies. At the 1972 Munich Olympics , a group of Arab terrorists known as Black September (a wing of Yasir Arafat's Al Fatah group) murdered eleven Israeli athletes as a way of drawing attention to their cause.

Julia Pascal, The Independent 21 September 2011

Honeypot: The startling story of the killer in heels
A new play about a female Mossad agent exposes the use of the 'honeytrap' in the Middle East.
She was tall, blonde and Swedish. The kind of woman who has known the adoration of men since adolescence. "Susanne" was in her fifties when I met her in Israel. She was Ingrid Bergman

and Liv Ullmann. I never guessed she was a Jew. Her atmosphere was sensuality and mystery. But, when I heard she had been a Mossad agent and a honeypot, I started asking questions.

The whispers from friends were that she had used her beauty as a tool to seduce Arab terrorists and kill them as they slept.

It was easy to see her appeal to Mossad. The stereotype shiksa is a blonde with no traditional semitic traits. Susanne had been a Swedish Protestant who converted to Judaism. When we met in the late 1980s, she had retired. She spoke to me about her reasons for joining Mossad. Learning about the Holocaust had traumatised her childhood. Watching footage of concentration camp survivors made her identify with the victims. This provoked her to go to Israel and be part of the struggle for the country's survival.

Susanne was part of Golda Meir's Operation Wrath of God in which teams of agents hunted down the members of the Palestinian group Black September responsible for assassinating 11 Israeli athletes at the 1972 Munich Olympics. Steven Spielberg's movie *Munich* partially explored these acts of revenge but no stage writer has yet portrayed how women were used in this dangerous operation.

The media picked up on Mossad's techniques in 1986 when Mordechai Vanunu exposed Israel's nuclear capacity to the press. Vanunu was seduced by agent "Cindy" in London. She promised him erotic nights in Italy but he was kidnapped by Mossad at Rome airport. At this time, Mossad, in common with most espionage agencies, continued to use honeypots. Tzipi Livni, current leader of Israel's opposition, worked for Mossad in Paris during the 1980s when my play is set. What she did is unknown.

The horror of the 1972 attack is still in Jewish memory. Abu Daoud masterminded these massacres. He claimed that the operation was financed by Mahmoud Abbas, now President of the Palestinian Authority. When Daoud died naturally in 2010, Abbas sent his condolences to the family. There has been no denial of this link.

Why is *Honeypot* relevant today? In London excitement is building for next summer's Olympics. But does the shadow of Munich remain in the collective memory? Newsreels from

1972 reveal that the Munich murders were an embarrassment to the Germans and the Olympic Committee who stopped the Games for only half a day. Requests by Israel for an official commemoration of the killings have continually been denied. I doubt if the London Organising Committee will honour the memory of the Israeli athletes.

The political mood has changed since 1972, but does the shadow of the Holocaust and Munich still leave a sense of unease? After all, the 1972 Games were also an act of resistance to Hitler's 1936 Munich Olympics as well as proof of Germany's improved post-Holocaust relationship with Israel.

Today Israel experiences its first anti-government demonstrations. All over the Arab world, there is a seismic shift. Internationally there is a guarded sense of optimism. The prospect of a Palestinian state allows many Israelis the possibility of an equal negotiating partner where land can be exchanged for peace.

Within this current political debate, *Honeypot* connects past and present through a dramatic exploration of one woman's journey into the Middle East revenge cycle. The real Susanne, who inspired me, died four years ago. Her legacy, like that of Abu Daoud, Golda Meir and Mahmoud Abbas, provokes disturbing questions around identity and violence. Questions which refuse to disappear.

Characters

SUSANNE/MIA ANDERSEN
35

KOBY ARIELI
Mossad Trainer, 50

JOSEPH ASSAD
A Palestinian, 50

The action is January-June, 1982.

The set can be simple or elaborate.

ACT ONE

SCENE ONE

SPOTLIGHT

CHURCH MUSIC. Hymns in Swedish.

SUSANNE in a spot.

PASTOR V/O: Dearly beloved. We are gathered together to celebrate an exceptional human being. Dr William Andersen brought many children on to this earth. A doctor is like a god but he is not a god. He performs God's will. The babies this man helped take their first breath are now men and women who may not know his name but he gave them the most precious gift of all. Life. This Church also gave him something precious. When he came to Sweden, he was a twelve year old fleeing those who hate God. He came to us for shelter and, in return, I asked him to take our Lord as his. *(SUSANNE looks up.)*

PASTOR: I did this because to convert a Jew is a holy act. It helps our Saviour return to our earth. Tell me, was I wrong to take a Jew to the one true faith? Won't he and I stand side by side at Judgment Day with the bright light of Jesus before us?

SUSANNE: A Jew?

PASTOR V/O: And the joy of eternity will be his forever.

SCENE TWO

SUSANNE is in hospital scrubs. She is unpacking a suitcase. There is a man's jacket. She smells her father's clothing and holds it to her.

SCENE THREE

SUSANNE is talking to her child

Darling Malena.

You going to sleep soon? You want momma to tell you a story?

Once upon a time there was a little girl called Malena who looked just like you with blonde hair and blue eyes. And she wanted to see her grandmother who lived far away in the woods. She was going to take her some honey. And on the way she saw a tall tree and a lovely bird at the top. She thought about climbing it but she's never dared do that before. She took one step and then another until she was high, high, high and the clouds all around were caressing her cheeks and the winds were playing with her curly hair. And the little bird, who had a lovely red breast, kept hopping all around her until he came so near that she could stroke his wings. And she said to him, 'Come closer dear little robin so that I can touch you all over!' And the bird came because he loved the music of her voice. And she lightly caressed his wing and she stroked his head and tickled behind his neck until he was cooing with delight. And then she said, come into my palm dear sweet bird so that I can tickle you even more. And he did because he so loved the little girl and all she was doing to him, his feathers all ruffled up and his chest all puffed out, and he sang and sang such sweet music that he put his neck between her fingers so that she could feel how he was throbbing with delight for her.

And then when he was singing his sweetest song his dear little heart suddenly stopped. The little girl grew afraid. Did she squeeze him too hard? You asleep Malena? My darling? Mummy is going away but just for a short while. Daddy will be here soon to kiss you goodnight. And Mummy will come back soon. Sleep Malena Sleep.

(Light change.)

(SUSANNE learns Hebrew.)

SUSANNE: *(Into a routine.)* Aleph, bet, gimmel, dalet, hey, vov, zain, het, tet, yod, kaf, lamed, mem, nun, samekh, ayin, pe, tsadi, gof,resh,shin, tav.

SCENE FOUR

Travelling.

Sound of the interior of a plane.

SUSANNE is dragging an old trunk across the stage.

V/O *(Israeli pilot)*: Ladies and gentlemen. This is your Captain speaking. As the sun rises over the land of Israel, we are about to land in Tel Aviv.

Please keep your seat belts fastened until the safety light has been switched off.

SOUND OF APPLAUSE.

SOUND OF THE ISRAELI STREET.

SCENE FIVE

SUSANNE & KOBY

An office in Tel Aviv. Israel. There is a jug of water and glasses on the table. KOBY is playing with a pack of cigarettes. They have been talking for some time.

KOBY: How did you find us?

SUSANNE: A man I knew.

KOBY: And what was his name?

SUSANNE: I don't remember. Shmuel. Shlomo.

KOBY: Schmuck. Why are you here?

SUSANNE: I told you. I want to do something for Israel.

He takes out matches and then decides not to smoke. It is clear this is a battle.

KOBY: *(Offers her one.)* At ohevet?[1]

SUSANNE: No. I don't.

KOBY: Smoking and cancer. The Nazis researched the links back in 1940s. Part of their 'healthy living' programme. I could die laughing! Why are you here?

---

1   You want?

SUSANNE: Personal reasons

KOBY: You got Mind Scratch?

SUSANNE: What's that?

KOBY: Brain itch. You can't eat, sleep or shit til you scratch it

SUSANNE: *(Playing with the words.)* Mind Scratch.

KOBY: Why are you here?

SUSANNE: It's not important.

KOBY: Everything is important.

SUSANNE: Believe me

KOBY: Everything. This is not an employment office. When we choose a woman we already know who she is. Her parents. Grandparents. Right back to Eve. We catch them young. When they join the army. They don't come knocking on the door. So Miss Sweden why do you want to join us?

SUSANNE: Sweden was neutral.

KOBY: And?

SUSANNE: The Nazi trains came through our country but nobody 'noticed'.

KOBY: You mean your parents flirted with them? So now you want to help the Jews?

SUSANNE: My parents did not do that.

KOBY: Oh the noble Swedes!

SUSANNE: But I know what you went through

KOBY: Are you one naïve girl!

SUSANNE: I'm a woman.

KOBY: Ayze Balagan!

SUSANNE: Just give me a chance. Please!

KOBY: Your name.

SUSANNE: Susanne Andersen.

SCENE SIX

KOBY: Name.

SUSANNE: Mia. Mia Larson.

KOBY: Where did you study?

SUSANNE: University of London. Modern Languages.

KOBY: You're Swedish. Why London?

SUSANNE: The best degree.

KOBY: Which college?

SUSANNE: UCL University College London.

KOBY: Which languages?

SUSANNE: Can we slow this a bit?

KOBY: *(Faster.)* Why did you become a journalist?

SUSANNE: My father ran a news agency in Stockholm.

KOBY: Who do you write for now?

SUSANNE: Freelance. The London Times.

KOBY: What do you write?

SUSANNE: Health. Infant mortality. The effect of climate on longevity. Rejuvenation.

KOBY: Monkey glands?

SUSANNE: Stem cell.

KOBY: Say more.

SUSANNE: Umbilical cords. Dead embryos.

KOBY: What are you doing in Paris?

SUSANNE: New research. Foetal cells for face creams.

KOBY: Why are you alone?

SUSANNE: I am waiting for a colleague.

KOBY: Who?

SUSANNE: A fellow journalist

KOBY: Why Paris?

SUSANNE: The French are tops for skin research.

KOBY: Children?

SUSANNE: No.

KOBY: Husband?

SUSANNE: No.

KOBY: *(For real now.)* OK. Tell me about him.

SUSANNE: Who?

KOBY: Your husband back in Stockholm.

SUSANNE: Mikael? Well he's a good guy. Practical.

KOBY: Job?

SUSANNE: Works for the town hall. Government planning.
Roads,
construction.

KOBY: How long are you married?

SUSANNE: Ten years.

KOBY: Your first boyfriend?

SUSANNE: No.

KOBY: You sleep around?

SUSANNE: Why do you ask?

KOBY: I have to know everything about you.

SUSANNE: Nobody knows everything about you.

KOBY: Not even your husband?

SUSANNE: And your wife?

KOBY: You sleep around.

SUSANNE: None of your business.

KOBY: There's the door. Shalom.

SUSANNE: *(Beat.)* How do you know? I dress modestly.

KOBY: That's not it.

SUSANNE: What then?

KOBY: It's what you give out. You've got someone else.

SUSANNE: Sex stops me feeling dead.

KOBY: Who?

SUSANNE: Nobody. An occasional encounter.

KOBY: *(Beat.)* There's nothing you can't say to me. No modesty, no shyness, you've got to be prepared for anything.

SUSANNE: *(Beat.)* There's someone I see.

KOBY: A lover?

SUSANNE: No. Not that. Just someone. We do it sometimes. There's nothing more.

KOBY: No?

SUSANNE: Sex stops me feeling dead.

KOBY: And with this boyfriend.

SUSANNE: Not boyfriend! We don't go out.

KOBY: And when you are with him you also think of other guys?

SUSANNE: How do you know?

KOBY: It's my job.

SUSANNE: I feel kind of guilty.

KOBY: Go on.

SUSANNE: Could be I remember a young guy I've met in the hospital. He wants me but I say no. Then I think of him when I am with this someone. I am unfaithful to my husband with this guy and, when he's in me, I'm thinking of this boy.

KOBY: *(Eat.)* Where is he? Mikael?

SUSANNE: Stockholm.

KOBY: What did you tell him?

SUSANNE: I'm away at a nursing conference.

KOBY: He can't know.

SUSANNE: He won't.

KOBY: And he believes you?

SUSANNE: He trusts me.

KOBY: *(Beat.)* He can never know.

SUSANNE: He won't.

KOBY: Do you love him?

SUSANNE: Of course.

KOBY: What do you love about him?

SUSANNE: The way he fixes things around the house.

KOBY: You fell in love with the caretaker?

SUSANNE: How dare you!

KOBY: *(Back to the interrogation.)* Name.

SUSANNE: Mia.

KOBY: Mother's maiden name?

SUSANNE: Sklar.

KOBY: Father's mother's maiden name?

SUSANNE: Olsen.

KOBY: Where did you go to school?

SUSANNE: Stockholm.

KOBY: Which?

SUSANNE: Bergundsskolan.

KOBY: Primary or Secondary?

SUSANNE: Primary.

KOBY: Address?

SUSANNE: Långholmsgatan 23

KOBY: Which languages did you study?

SUSANNE: French. English.

KOBY: You didn't say Swedish.

SUSANNE: Would you say Hebrew?

KOBY: Good. You missed one.

SUSANNE: Did I?

KOBY: German.

SUSANNE: All Swedes speak German.

KOBY: *Klum.*

SUSANNE: I'm not stupid.

KOBY: Get out of here.

SUSANNE: Why?

KOBY: *Klum*'s Hebrew.

SUSANNE: For 'stupid'. Shit.

KOBY: Or did you forget?

(Losing it.)

You come here. You beg me to use you. You don't say why? You think this is some kind of game? You think you can waste my time? You think I sit here all day pushing people around and this will be some kind of kick for me? Well let me tell you lady? I've seen too many women want to get into this. They think it's exciting. They think they'll get high. Make history. But it's waiting and schwitzing, it's boring and it's hateful. There's nothing glamorous or Mata Hari. So you know what I think. I think you should get yourself a little tour of the country. Take a trip to the Dead Sea. Get yourself a mud bath and then wash all this Jew-shit out of your hair and go back home to your nice little country.

(SUSANNE leaves angrily. He goes to pick up the phone.)

SCENE SEVEN

TWO HOURS LATER.

(KOBY is eating at his desk. SUSANNE comes in.)

KOBY: So there's plane strike on Swedish Airways?

SUSANNE: I'm not going anywhere. I told you what I want

KOBY: Yeh, do something for Israel.

SUSANNE: Don't you believe me?

KOBY: You want some falafel? There's not much left.

SUSANNE: I'm not hungry

KOBY: And that's a reason not to eat? *(Beat.)* Why are you back here?

This is not for you.

SUSANNE: I told you.

KOBY: Because you're Swedish. Because you were born too late? What do you know? You're a Protestant. You never knew a Jew in your life.

SUSANNE: I came to Israel.

KOBY: And what? You fucked some Israeli.

SUSANNE: I met people with numbers on their arms.

KOBY: And you liked his dick? You're not Wallenberg.

SUSANNE: No but I've got something valuable.

KOBY: Oh yes?

SUSANNE: I can pass

KOBY: As a shiksa

SUSANNE: What's that?

KOBY: What every Arab and Jew wants. A blonde doll.

SUSANNE: Is that how you see me?

KOBY: Only on the outside. Inside you've got to be a smart Jew.

SUSANNE: So let me do something Jewish.

KOBY: Oh a righteous gentile.[2]

SUSANNE: Like Jesus?

---

2   The concept of the Righteous Gentile was used after The Holocaust to depict someone who is not Jewish and who helped Jews escape from annihilation.

KOBY: Another meschugennah Jew.[3]

SUSANNE: You gave him up.

KOBY: Yeh and for this we paid times six million.[4] *(Beat.)*

I like you. *(She looks at him.)* I mean it.

SUSANNE: Good.

KOBY: Not good.

SUSANNE: Why?

KOBY: You're not cut out for this.

SUSANNE: You hear about the cockroach theory?

KOBY: What?

SUSANNE: You're in your apartment and shit, look at those! Thousands of them. So you get out the gas canister and you spray here and there and over and over until they're gone. And then wow you can breathe, that's it. A year later, you're in the kitchen, it's the middle of the night, you turn on the light and, there they are. First you see two then there's more, hundreds of them, maybe thousands. They're back and shit you can never get rid of them. That's how the world thinks about the Jews.

KOBY: Now you sound like an Israeli.

Lights down. Lights up. Time has passed.

SCENE EIGHT

KOBY: Give me your day.

SUSANNE: I get up at five. I'm on the ward at seven.

KOBY: Why did you want to be a nurse?

SUSANNE: My father was a doctor

KOBY: What kind?

SUSANNE: Gynaecology and obstetrics.

3   Meschugenah is Yiddish (and also German) for crazy.
4   An ironic reference to the six million Jews who died in The Holocaust.

KOBY: And you do what?

SUSANNE: Gynaecology and obstetrics.

KOBY: Daddy's girl. *(She turns away.)*

KOBY: What's the matter?

SUSANNE: Nothing.

KOBY: You're upset.

SUSANNE: No.

KOBY: What is it with your father?

SUSANNE: Nothing.

KOBY: Where is he?

SUSANNE: Dead.

KOBY: When?

SUSANNE: Three months ago.

KOBY: Nine to go.

SUSANNE: What?

KOBY: A year of mourning. Nine months left. Enough to have a child.

SUSANNE: What are you talking about?

KOBY: Your father.

SUSANNE: I don't want to go there.

KOBY: You don't want, you don't want? You come here and you want to dictate the rules?

SUSANNE: Sorry.

KOBY: You get to the hospital at seven. When are you in theatre?

SUSANNE: Seven thirty.

KOBY: And? What's the usual?

SUSANNE: D and C. Scrape. Hysterectomy.

KOBY: What's that?

SUSANNE: Clearing out the uterus. Or ripping it out.

KOBY: You're angry with me. Good.

SUSANNE: I came to do a job.

KOBY: And I am doing mine. Your father?

SUSANNE: No.

KOBY: Where is he?

SUSANNE: Lying under a cross.

KOBY: Why are you angry?

SUSANNE: Because he's dead.

KOBY: Your mother?

SUSANNE: Also dead.

KOBY: What was she like?

SUSANNE: Ok.

KOBY: You don't want to go there.

SUSANNE: Nothing to say.

KOBY: You come in here straight from Stockholm. You won't tell me shit.

I don't know you, I can't use you. *(Holding cigarette.)* My wife Nurit wants me to give these up. After thirty years marriage. I could sleep with every pretty girl soldier in the Israeli army and she wouldn't give a damn but this, this is important to her. She wants to keep me alive.

SUSANNE: She's right.

KOBY: *(Beat.)* Some agents go crazy. You'll never be the same. You lie in bed. You feel the air move. You shoot. Problem is when you go back home and the kid comes into the bed. *(She looks away. He looks at her).* You lied, you have a child.

SUSANNE: A daughter.

KOBY: Lie better. But the next time you lie to me I put you on the plane myself. *(Beat.)* How old?

SUSANNE: Eighteen months.

KOBY: Walking?

SUSANNE: Not yet.

KOBY: Shit.

SUSANNE: Don't tell me all your women agents are childless.

KOBY: We know who they are. You are off the streets.

SUSANNE: I'm clean *(Phone rings. It is his boss.)*

KOBY: Ma? Matai? Eyfor?[5] OK *(Back to her.)* Come with me.

SCENE NINE

On the waterfront. Tel Aviv.

KOBY: Be my wife. *(SUSANNE puts her arm through his.)*

KOBY: Chatichat!

SUSANNE: What's that?

KOBY: What Israeli men call women like you. A dish.

SUSANNE: Chatichat.

KOBY: You've got to get the ch sound. Like you're about to spit.

SUSANNE: You're funny.

KOBY: A pretty woman can go for an ugly man as long as he's funny.

SUSANNE: Who told you that?

KOBY: An ugly bitch!

SUSANNE: Were you born here?

KOBY: I'm a sabra.

SUSANNE: What's that?

KOBY: Like a cactus. Prickly on the outside.

SUSANNE: *(Beat.)* And on the inside?

KOBY: You flirting with me?

SUSANNE: I never flirt. Why do the men here wear open-necked shirts, not ties? They all look like my father.

---

5   Hebrew for What? Where? When?

KOBY: Did he come here?

SUSANNE: Why would he?

KOBY: The Jesus Trail. Nazareth. Bethlehem.

SUSANNE: No.

KOBY: What did he think of Jews?

SUSANNE: I don't know.

KOBY: You didn't tell me his name.

SUSANNE: William.

KOBY: *(As if noting it.)* William Andersen. Look over there to the left where you see rocks. That's Jaffa. Where the British stopped the survivors coming into the country. You been to London?

SUSANNE: Paris. I was an au pair. Just seventeen. Couple of months.

Apartment in la Rue de l'Estrapade. Near Le Panthéon on the Left Bank. The father was called Gunther. An East German Communist. Spoke no French. First night I got there he made me go to the pharmacy with him to ask for something that would kill his crabs.

I gave him the lotion and then I heard him screaming in the bathroom.

KOBY: Where is he now?

SUSANNE: Still in Paris I guess.

KOBY: What was he doing there?

SUSANNE: I never thought to ask. It was so long ago.

KOBY: Gunther what?

SUSANNE: Baumgarten.

KOBY: *(Beat.)* Long square face, blue eyes. Thin. Late forties. Lots of trips to Beirut.

(SUSANNE looks amazed.)

KOBY: What if we need you to meet Gunther again?

SUSANNE: Warum nicht?[6]

SCENE TEN

SUSANNE is alone. She is playing a tape recorder. She stops it and replays it when she needs. It is the voice of her Hebrew teacher. During this scene she is trying on outfits. She changes from hospital scrubs to prettier clothes. The changing is to show her move from her past to her future work.

TEACHER V/O: So yes Susanne you can record this and revise it for the next lesson.

Basic Ivrit.

Woman. Isha.

Mother. Ima

Shalom.

SUSANNE: Peace. Hello. Goodbye.

TEACHER V/O: Now I ask the question and we leave a space for you to answer.

Woman?

SUSANNE: Isha. No! Ima. No Isha.

TEACHER V/O: Friend?

SUSANNE: Chaver. Friends. Chaverim!

TEACHER V/O: Bitay Avon?

SUSANNE: Bitay avon. Enjoy your meal! Bon Appetit!

TEACHER V/O: Eretz Israel?[7]

SUSANNE: Something Israel. Eretz?

TEACHER V/O: Boker tov?

SUSANNE: Good morning

TEACHER V/O: Lila Tov?

SUSANNE: Good night.

TEACHER V/O: Father?

---

6   German for Why not.
7   This means the land of Israel.

SUSANNE: Father? Father? I don't know. I don't know.

SCENE ELEVEN

THE OFFICE.

KOBY: I need to see if you can act.

SUSANNE: Now?

KOBY: Now. *(Beat.)* Do it!

SUSANNE: I'm in the hotel this morning and there's this American Israeli. Maybe 60. Talking to this other woman maybe 50.

(She 'acts' both voices. They intercut with one another fast.)

AMERICAN: I mean my mother she never had a line on her face but my father, see this, *(Pointing to between her eyebrows.)* just like him. *(To the woman opposite.)* You sure you never had a face lift?

ENGLISH: Oh I was a Zionist back then. Going to Israel in 1967 and up to the Wall in Jerusalem. And God we felt proud. It was our country.

KOBY: Carry on. More.

AMERICAN: And your neck and chest, look it doesn't have those criss – cross lines at all.

ENGLISH: We were home. Here was where we felt we belonged. Then it started to go bad.

AMERICAN: Now your hair so thick and curly. My husband doesn't like that I straighten mine, well he's Chinese.

ENGLISH: The land they said was empty because we got rid of who was there before.

AMERICAN: What you English need is a French Revolution.

ENGLISH: And I know yes when your house is burning you jump out the window…

AMERICAN: To Palestine.

ENGLISH: …and you land on the poor guy in the street.

KOBY: *(Slow handclap.)* You should be at the Habimah.

SUSANNE: What's that?

KOBY: Jewish national theatre. Shouting, shouting, always shouting. Why do Jews always have to shout? *(Beat.)* Now, I say something you react.

SUSANNE: OK.

KOBY: 1967.

SUSANNE: Six Day War.

KOBY: Your opinion?

SUSANNE: You don't give back what you gained.

KOBY: What are you? A Christian Zionist?

SUSANNE: Israel's a tiny country. I thought it was massive til I came here.

It's a pawn. The Soviets support the Arabs. The Americans Israel.

KOBY: And how do you know all this?

SUSANNE: I read. I listen. I believe that Jews deserve their own country. And anyone who stops them has to learn that.

KOBY: Some people would say we have enough and why do we need the West Bank? Gaza?

SUSANNE: Security. Jews have been almost wiped out by Christian Europe. And now it's not safe to trust anyone.

KOBY: Menachim Begin[8] would love you!

SUSANNE: I hate politics.

KOBY: Why?

SUSANNE: They're all crooks.

KOBY: *(Back to the role play.)* Jews?

SUSANNE: Don't know any.

KOBY: You should know one or two.

8   Menachim Begin. Founder of the right-wing Likud Party and Israel's sixth Prime Minister 1977-1983.

SUSANNE: University. I lived way out. The Jewish girl I shared a house with. Drove into town everyday anyway. Charged me for petrol. Mean bitch.

KOBY: Know any Arabs?

SUSANNE: Once I had a boyfriend from Iran. Bahram. Hated the Shah and then Khomeni.

KOBY: Iranians aren't Arabs!

SUSANNE: *(Embarrassed.)* Of course!

KOBY: You never had a Moroccan boyfriend back in Paris?

SUSANNE: *(Catching on.)* Yes. Nabil. He was very cute. And circumcised.

KOBY: Africa? India? Backpacking?

SUSANNE: No.

KOBY: Name.

SUSANNE: Mia.

KOBY: Mother's maiden name?

SUSANNE: I told you.

KOBY: Father's mother's maiden name?

SUSANNE: Olsen.

KOBY: Where did you go to school?

SUSANNE: I need a break.

KOBY: No break.

SUSANNE: A question.

KOBY: What?

SUSANNE: If Jews are so smart why didn't they see what would happen when they kicked the Arabs out?

KOBY: In 1948 there was time to think ahead? You think Jews from the camps had time to live like hippies? Go back to Stockholm Susanne. You're confused.

SUSANNE: No, I am not. I am here and I am ready to fight.

KOBY: *Go to Palestine* they said in the 1930s. Now they say *Get Out Of Palestine*. Are you any different?

SUSANNE: Stop making me the enemy.

KOBY: What are you?

SUSANNE: Anything you want.

KOBY: Tell me why.

SUSANNE: Because my mother was a failed mother and a hysteric? Is that what you're going to put in your psychological report? That doing something for Israel is my way of getting back at her? Look I'm here because I want to leave a mark. To right a wrong. The world hates Jews and Israel.

KOBY: You're not a Jew. Why do you care?

SUSANNE: Define a Jew.

KOBY: Someone with a Jewish mother.

SUSANNE: I'm not a Jew.

KOBY: What are you?

SUSANNE: What the hell does that mean?

KOBY: What drives you lady? What brings you half way across the world to a country you don't know on a mission that might kill you? Are you a crazy? We got plenty of those. We got guys coming to Jerusalem they think they're Jesus. We got mental wards full of them. We got women who think they're Jesus' mother or his wife, or his auntie. We got a whole country of meschugennahs[9]. I need to be sure you're not one of them. You come here looking for what lady? You want to save the Jews! Well it's too late. We got five thousand years talking to God. And the guy wasn't listening. And where does it all end. In the ash! No damned saviour came down from heaven to help us so now we have to make it up as we go along. And you, who the hell are you? This is dangerous work. You fuck this up

---

9   Crazy people.

and we all go to hell. So tell me something to convince me.
Or get the hell out of here.

SUSANNE: You think I know? I don't. *(Beat.)* When I got off
the plane and walked down the steps, this wave of heat
hit me. And when it did something changed. Something is
pulling me here and I don't know what it is *(Pause.)* Back
home. In the labour ward. Sometimes there's a woman
with uterine cancer. She knows she is going to die soon and
she is giving birth! She wills herself to live long enough
to push out this blood and slime-covered animal. Me, I
don't have that type of guts. But here, in this country I
understand her. Me? I'm healthy I have a daughter but
inside I'm dead. Like those men and women walking down
Allenby Street with numbers on their arms. I've got to
make something live.

What more do you want from me?

(Pause. He is considering.)

KOBY: You go to the Academy for training.

SUSANNE: Where?

KOBY: Herzlya. Near the Country Club. On the Haifa Road.

SUSANNE: Where will I work?

KOBY: Abroad.

SUSANNE: What?

KOBY: 'The Office' doesn't work in Israel.

SUSANNE: 'The Office'?

KOBY: *(Beat.)* We'll give you a virgin passport. You obey
orders.

SUSANNE: And you. What's your story?

KOBY: Don't even go there

SUSANNE: Why not?

KOBY: If you're caught.

SUSANNE: You think I'll talk?

KOBY: With enough pain everyone talks.

SUSANNE: OK.

KOBY: These guys you fuck. You meet them where? At the gym?

SUSANNE: I said there was one. Singular.

KOBY: But that's only half the story, isn't it. *(Silence.)*

If you keep things back I can't use you.

SUSANNE: I've never told anyone. *(Beat.)* It's just sex.

(Self-mocking.) Man's brain, woman's body!

KOBY: *(Beat.)* Where? In the locker room?

SUSANNE: Gym is gym. Fucking is fucking. *(Beat.)*

KOBY: In the hospital?

(Beat.) So that's where you meet the fucks.

SUSANNE: They're men!

KOBY: So sensitive! Patients?

SUSANNE: I don't break the rules.

KOBY: Colleagues?

SUSANNE: Sometimes.

KOBY: Doctors?

SUSANNE: Occasionally.

KOBY: And?

SUSANNE: They tell me stuff.

KOBY: What?

SUSANNE: Genetic testing. Poisons.

KOBY: Such as?

SUSANNE: Toxins that kill only one ethnic group.

KOBY: South African data. What else do they tell you?

SUSANNE: Smart dust.

KOBY: You know about that?

SUSANNE: Data picked up in dust. Microdot microphones. That's really something.

KOBY: Who tells you this?

SUSANNE: Guys from the Balkans. Serbs, Croats, Bosnians.

KOBY: You're a regular little UN. Who else?

SUSANNE: Iraqi doctors who got out.

KOBY: You fuck them?

SUSANNE: I don't need to.

KOBY: For us that could change. That bother you?

SUSANNE: No.

KOBY: We have to be sure.

SUSANNE: I'm here to do a job.

KOBY: *(Beat.)* There's a guy.

SUSANNE: What guy?

KOBY: Munich. The Olympics

SUSANNE: Oh.

KOBY: Our best athletes. Machine-gunned. Burned alive on the airport runway. 1972. The Olympics nobody wants to talk about. And when the Arabs took our boys, what did we do? We listened to the Germans. We did everything they wanted like fucking concentration camp prisoners. The Arabs kill the Jews overnight and the next day the Germans restart The Games. If our guys had been blacks from the Third World, there'd be a ceremony with every Olympic opening. But hell we mustn't upset the Arabs.

SUSANNE: What do I do?

KOBY: You become an athlete too.

SUSANNE: What does that mean?

KOBY: You train and you train and you train. Those bastards, we didn't get them all. In Sweden, we fucked up, 'The Office' killed a Moroccan waiter.

SUSANNE: And who said all Jews were smart!

45

KOBY: This guy you're assigned to…

SUSANNE: Did he kill?

KOBY: He's the brains behind it all.

SUSANNE: Shit

KOBY: That's why he has to be removed.

SUSANNE: Who is he?

KOBY: He's Robert and Rémy, He's John and Zaid, he's Anthony and Keith. Whatever you need, he becomes. This guy, he's smart. He picks up new languages like you buy new clothes. He's a business man, a journalist, a doctor. Your best friend and your uncle. He's the father you never had. The lover you always desired. For ten years we've been hunting and when we get close he vanishes.

SUSANNE: What does he look like?

KOBY: Whichever new face he's bought in Budapest or Istanbul.

SUSANNE: How will I know him?

KOBY: We'll show you recent photos.

SUSANNE: When?

KOBY: When we think you're ready.

SUSANNE: How will I meet him?

KOBY: We'll tell you. But you have to wait.

SUSANNE: Long?

KOBY: Long enough for me to know you.

SCENE ELEVEN

SUSANNE is learning Hebrew and her vocabulary is on double-sided cards. Hebrew and English.

SUSANNE: *Abba.* Daddy. Father. William. Werner. Susanne. Mia. Berlin. Stockholm. German. Bosch. Kraut. Hebrew. *Ivrit.* Jew. Yid. Kaddish. Only the man says kaddish. *(Angry.)* A girl doesn't count. *Klum.* Stupid. *Shalom.* Peace!

Anee lor medaberet Ivrit. I don't speak Hebrew. *Sheket.* Shut Up. *Chai.* Life. *L'Chaim.* To life. *Ish.* Man. *Isha* Woman. *Kol Isha.* A woman's voice. *Mazel.* Luck. *Tov.* Good. *Mazel Tov.* Good Luck. Werner wish me luck!

SCENE TWELVE

GUN TRAINING.

SUSANNE is alone. She has a gun in her hand. She is wearing ear protection and goggles. She is practising target shooting. KOBY enters. He stands behind her to guide her. At times his arms are around her waist. He is training her and there is a hint of sexuality.

KOBY: Weight on two feet. Root yourself.

SUSANNE: Like this?

KOBY: Good girl.

SUSANNE: *(Admires the gun and the language of the gun.)* Beretta 71. Point 2.2. Rim fire. Perfect

KOBY: Breathe. Relax. *(She does.)*

SUSANNE: A nine millimetre has a heavier calibre but the point two two gives a quieter discharge. *(She turns to him.)* Why not a rifle?

KOBY: A point two two rifle could kill from a mile away. It's got advantages, We call it 'The Whispering Killer'. But there's more chance of a miss. Or the bullet goes straight through the target's soft tissue. Or into some American tourist. Go close range, then, no emotion. You're sure of a hit.

SUSANNE: Right. I have to shoot into the largest body mass.

KOBY: Why?

SUSANNE: Shock to the internal organs.

KOBY: Your job is?

SUSANNE: Bullet to the brain. Straight into the skull. Base. *(She looks at him.)*

KOBY: Scared? You can pull out now.

SUSANNE: I said I'll do it.

KOBY: When he's tired the reflexes are slow. Best is after sex, Three a.m., four. He's asleep. Even if he wakes he's spent. This is it!

SUSANNE: His flesh all over me. I clean myself fast. Don't look back. Run!

KOBY: Do it! *(She fires three times.)*

SCENE THIRTEEN

KOBY and SUSANNE.

KOBY: Tell me.

SUSANNE: What?

KOBY: Your first experience.

SUSANNE: Why?

KOBY: Your body is a weapon. Look you can't be shy with me.

SUSANNE: I'm not.

KOBY: You want this job or are you playing ?

SUSANNE: This Zaid, this Rémy, this Kevin, this Keith, this Arab chameleon, he likes women?

KOBY: Yes.

SUSANNE: You sent others?

KOBY: He'd smell a Jew.

SUSANNE: And that's why you haven't thrown me out? *(Pause.)*

KOBY: Tell me about the first time.

SUSANNE: OK. I'm sixteen. I've been dating for a month.

KOBY: And?

SUSANNE: I want to get rid of my virginity.

KOBY: Who was he?

SUSANNE: A guy I met in a club. First time is supposed to be crap. It wasn't.

KOBY: Sex is important to you?

SUSANNE: Yes.

KOBY: So you understand what it means to men?

SUSANNE: I think so.

KOBY: What do you think guys like?

SUSANNE: Every man is different.

KOBY: You have to read him.

SUSANNE: Meaning?

KOBY: Guess his secret. What does he want most? *(Beat.)* Let's start with your husband. What does he like?

SUSANNE: Me talking about my fantasies

KOBY: And?

SUSANNE: You want to know?

KOBY: Don't worry. I don't turn on.

SUSANNE: Don't you?

KOBY: I'm listening.

SUSANNE: I'm in a small space.

KOBY: Like what? A cupboard? A toilet?

SUSANNE: Like a lift.

KOBY: What?

SUSANNE: An elevator. And the doors close. There's just him and me.

KOBY: Who is he?

SUSANNE: I don't know. No talking, no names.

KOBY: What does he look like?

SUSANNE: Italian. Indian. Dark. Foreign.

KOBY: Arab?

SUSANNE: Maybe.

KOBY: You speak?

SUSANNE: No.

KOBY: What happens?

SUSANNE: He puts his hand on my breast.

KOBY: And?

SUSANNE: He raises my skirt.

KOBY: Then?

SUSANNE: The lift door opens and another man comes in.

KOBY: Yes?

SUSANNE: The second guy. He gets excited, watches us doing it.

KOBY: And what's he like.

SUSANNE: Foreign but different.

KOBY: And?

SUSANNE: He caresses my breasts.

KOBY: Who?

SUSANNE: The second guy.

KOBY: What's the first one doing?

SUSANNE: Inside me.

KOBY: Two guys at once?

SUSANNE: No. One doing and one kissing.

KOBY: Then?

SUSANNE: A woman comes in.

KOBY: Who?

SUSANNE: The first guy's wife.

KOBY: And?

SUSANNE: She watches.

KOBY: What?

SUSANNE: I watch her watching me with her husband.

KOBY: What's she doing?

SUSANNE: She's frozen.

KOBY: And you watch her?

SUSANNE: Yes.

KOBY: And you like that!

SUSANNE: How do you know?

KOBY: It makes you triumphant.

SUSANNE: Yes!

KOBY: Tell me more.

SUSANNE: I like them to be married.

KOBY: Why?

SUSANNE: I don't want them falling in love.

KOBY: And being married stops that?

SUSANNE: It stops them leaving their wife.

KOBY: I can see why guys like you. What do you enjoy?

SUSANNE: When they move with you and it's kind of a wave you both ride.

KOBY: What do you feel?

SUSANNE: Like I'm going to another country. With no name. Where I've never been.

KOBY: Like you are now.

SUSANNE: What?

KOBY: On your face.

SUSANNE: What?

KOBY: I don't know what words to use. Some kind of promise.

SUSANNE: What?

KOBY: That's what you have to offer. Your job is to let him think he's making the running. Be hot. Be cold. Never be easy.

SUSANNE: I never am.

KOBY: You have to be ready to do anything. *(Beat.)* What does your vagina mean to you?

SUSANNE: *(Beat.)* Nothing.

KOBY: Not true. It's where the world begins! That's true for him too. Every second he's thinking how he'll do it. Think about it. Make it happen. *(She closes her eyes.)*

Good. Now you feel it and so do I.

SUSANNE: You!

KOBY: I'm a guy, you've got to work me. Now open your eyes.

(She does.) Look at me and talk to me about something but, in your head, think about that feeling. Focus on there. Where you're most excited. That feeling is the same for him because every second he's thinking of what he'll do for you. Just him in you. Think about it. Make it happen!

SUSANNE: In Stockholm the sun is high late at night all through the summer

KOBY: Imagine him moving as you talk *(She closes her eyes.)*

SUSANNE: ......and you never want to sleep.

KOBY: Good.

SUSANNE: ......and your clothes feel heavy.

KOBY: Good.

SUSANNE: ......and there is the sun and the stars.

KOBY: That's it!!

SUSANNE: ......and your skin feels light And the quality of the light is quite different from the light in any other city.

KOBY: Mia!

SUSANNE: *(Opens her eyes.)* Yes!

SCENE FOURTEEN

THE PHONE CALL HOME.

SUSANNE: Hello. Mikael. Yes it's me. I'm in London with a girlfriend. No I'm not seeing anyone else. There's only you. How are you? I miss you too. And Malena? Don't say that. Tell her I'll be home soon. Did she! She said Daddy! That's wonderful! Soon she'll say Mummy. Of course I'll be back to hear it. No! Why would you think that?

(Sound of someone shouting in Hebrew. 'Hurry up with the phone will you!')

I'm in London I told you. Is your mother taking Malena sometimes? No of course I don't think you're no good. You're a wonderful father and I'm a terrible mother. Let me talk to her. Malena! I want you to be a good girl and I'll soon be home to tell you a bedtime story. And when I'm home I'll hold you so hard you'll forget I ever left. Say Mummy. Go on. Say it darling. *(Dialling tone.)*

SCENE FIFTEEN

A SPOT ON SUSANNE

She remembers all the voices of all the interrogations she has endured in her training. The scene is played with her violently pulling on and off a dress.

V/O: Who were you talking to?

SUSANNE: Nobody.

V/O: I don't believe you.

SUSANNE: And it's none of your business.

V/O: Who were you calling?

V/O: Name?

SUSANNE: Who are you?

V/O: You want me to hit you again?

SUSANNE: No!

V/O: I want your name.

SUSANNE: Mia.

V/O: Mia who?

SUSANNE: Andersen.

V/O: Yeh like Hans Christian!

SUSANNE: It's true.

V/O: Where do you work?

SUSANNE: The US.

V/O: Where?

SUSANNE: The US.

V/O: You said London.

SUSANNE: No!

V/O: What paper?

SUSANNE: A health magazine.

V/O: Name?

SUSANNE: Live Longer.

V/O: Phone number?

SUSANNE: 793 2378.

V/O: City?

SUSANNE: Chicago.

V/O: Area code?

SUSANNE: What?

V/O: You don't even know the area code?

SUSANNE: I do.

V/O: You don't know?

SUSANNE: I do.

V/O: You don't know? Because Live Longer doesn't exist!
    Now tell me who you really are!

V/O: I have a gun. *(He clicks a gun.)* It's against your head. Can you feel it? You going to tell me who you are or I'm going to fire. You have a daughter.

SUSANNE: No!

V/O: You tell me your name or she gets the shot.

SUSANNE: Go to hell!

V/O: You take her to her nanny.

SUSANNE: I have no daughter!

V/O: Every morning at six.

SUSANNE: I told you.

V/O: I know her name!

V/O: Wake up!

SUSANNE: When will I sleep?

V/O: When I'm through.

SUSANNE: And food?

KOBY: Wake up Susanne!!!!

SCENE SEVENTEEN

SUSANNE: It was humiliating! Why did you bring my daughter into it?

KOBY: You think she is safe once you get into this. Or your husband. You want to get out now?

SUSANNE: No.

KOBY: We'll put five thousand into your Stockholm account. There will be no trace of where it comes from.

SUSANNE: I don't want it.

KOBY: Hotels in Rome, Paris, maybe London. Not cheap.

SUSANNE: You can pay for my expenses.

KOBY: You come to us. You don't want money. You want to fight for Israel. You're not a Jew or a crazy Zionist Christian. What is it? It doesn't make sense.

SUSANNE: I told you. I believe in your country. Or maybe it's that fucking mind-scratch. *(He plays with a box of matches.)* When is it to be?

KOBY: Very soon.

SUSANNE: Good.

KOBY: The point of no return

SUSANNE: Koby, I'm ready, I've been waiting all my life to do this. It's what I want in here *(Thumps heart.)* and with every cell in my body.

KOBY: There's something you're not telling me. You tell me or you get out of here and you never come back.

SUSANNE: *(Beat.)* What if my father was a Jew? *(Silence.)*

KOBY: So that's it! From where?

SUSANNE: Poland.

KOBY: Poland. Always Poland. And what?

SUSANNE: His parents.

KOBY: Your grandparents. Did they survive?

(Silence.)

You don't say much

SUSANNE: I said Poland.

KOBY: Where?

SUSANNE: Does it matter?

KOBY: Everything matters. Your father. What was his name?

SUSANNE: Werner Goldenberg and he lived his whole life as William Andersen.

KOBY: And his parents were gassed? What is this? You fighting some battle you think was his? What is this? You kill an Arab you think you killing a Nazi?

SUSANNE: Of course not. *(Beat.)* He should have come here.

KOBY: And the British should've opened the doors and your grandparents would have lived. *(Takes a cigarette and takes*

out his light. He tries to make it work but there is no petrol in it.)
You going to tell me about Werner's parents then?

SUSANNE: Treblinka.

KOBY: Treblinka to Tel Aviv. You're home.

SUSANNE: Is this my home?

KOBY: It could be.

SUSANNE: I see them every day when I wake up. And all night
in my head. I am piecing it together. My grandparents.
They gave their son a German name because they admired
the Germans! I see them pressed against one another
in the packed cattle car. The old lady wants to piss. She
can't because all the other people crushed against her are
watching. Such a proud woman and when she can't hold it
any longer she does it standing up and she's ashamed.

And me. I want to make all those dead Jews disappear.
(Beat.) I've copied my father! Just like him I spend my
days and nights bringing life into the world. Push! Push!
Push! Baby's coming! Why isn't that enough?

KOBY: *(Moved.)* Your daughter. Don't you want her say *mamma
I miss you*

SUSANNE: I must do this!

KOBY: Ever heard of André Schpitzer?

SUSANNE: Not sure.

KOBY: Born in Romania. Came here as a child. When he was
growing up, he had a dream. To walk under the Star of
David at the Munich Olympics.

SUSANNE: I like that.

KOBY: This guy, he was a fencing coach. When he got to
Munich he went up to the Lebanese athletes and made
friends with them. He believed in peace.

SUSANNE: Sounds good

KOBY: He watched the Palestinians throw a grenade into their
room and burn his friends alive and then they shot him.

SUSANNE: I got it.

KOBY: What's it like for his daughter growing up knowing her father was executed by Arab terrorists? A little girl like yours. What's her name again?

SUSANNE: You know!

KOBY: You say it.

SUSANNE: Malena

KOBY: Beautiful. Well this André, he was killed just for being a Jew. Not even a soldier. Just an ordinary guy who wants to win a medal. And he has a daughter who never got to know her father.

SUSANNE: What's her name?

KOBY: Never mind her name. You leave tomorrow!

SUSANNE: Tomorrow?

KOBY: So get the hell out of here.

(Interval.)

ACT TWO

SCENE SEVENTEEN

Paris a bar in a smart hotel. Sound of French voices.

JOE is drinking. He looks at Susanne who is reading Le Monde.

JOE: Excusez-moi?

SUSANNE: Oui?

JOE: Vous parlez anglais? Mademoiselle? Madame?

SUSANNE: Oui je parle anglais.

JOE: That's a relief.

SUSANNE: Yes?

JOE: The French are so, you know, French.

SUSANNE: Yes!

JOE: Would you like a drink?

SUSANNE: Do I look thirsty?

JOE: Yes.

SUSANNE: OK.

JOE: Whisky?

SUSANNE: Vodka. If it's cold.

JOE: Bison?

SUSANNE: Bison.

JOE: Let me guess.

SUSANNE: What?

JOE: Where you're from?

SUSANNE: OK.

JOE: The United States?

SUSANNE: No.

JOE: England?

SUSANNE: No.

JOE: Germany?

SUSANNE: No.

JOE: Sweden?

SUSANNE: Bull's eye. *(SUSANNE thumps her palm with her fist.)*

JOE: *(Playing with the phrase.)* Bull's eye. Sweden. Now, what do I know about Sweden? There was a story someone told me once. Is it Swedish or Norwegian? There are a lot of nobles sitting at a long table in a hall, hundreds and hundreds of years ago. And suddenly the huge doors of the medieval hall open to let in someone important. And, as the heavy wooden door opens, in flies a sparrow, and it flies the full length of the hall over the heads of all the people who are eating at this banquet. Then someone opens the other door and out it goes. Just like the human soul, a short flight and out into the sky. *(Silence.)*

What's a pretty lady doing alone at a hotel bar?

SUSANNE: *(Looking round.)* Where?

JOE: You are funny.

SUSANNE: Am I?

JOE: You drink alone?

SUSANNE: I'm waiting for someone.

JOE: Oh.

SUSANNE: A colleague.

JOE: A boyfriend?

SUSANNE: A colleague.

JOE: You're a married woman?

SUSANNE: Are you always so forward with strangers?

JOE: Forgive me.

SUSANNE: And you're a married man.

JOE: How do you know?

SUSANNE: You took your ring off !

JOE: You see the sun betrays me! *(Lifts his left hand to examine his ring finger. There's a white band where a ring was.)*

SUSANNE: And where's your wife?

JOE: At home.

SUSANNE: With her boyfriend?

JOE: I'd kill her.

SUSANNE: Of course.

JOE: And your husband?

SUSANNE: At home too.

JOE: What's he like?

SUSANNE: You do get in personal.

JOE: I'm a curious guy.

SUSANNE: It's OK.

JOE: So? He's in Stockholm. With the children?

SUSANNE: There are no children.

JOE: Sorry to hear that.

SUSANNE: Why sorry?

JOE: A woman's destiny.

SUSANNE: Is it?

JOE: In my culture.

SUSANNE: In all cultures. Take the uterus. Throw away the rest.

JOE: *(Beat.)* I never heard a woman talk like this.

SUSANNE: Where have you been living? *(Pause. It seems he might go. She is looking directly at him. He is intrigued by her boldness.)*

JOE: What's he like?

SUSANNE: Who?

JOE: Your husband?

SUSANNE: A sweet guy. Cooks me dinner.

JOE: Really?

SUSANNE: You look surprised. He's a better cook.

JOE: And your husband. He lets his wife travel. Alone?

SUSANNE: I have a meeting.

JOE: With?

SUSANNE: Another journalist.

JOE: A free woman.

SUSANNE: What does that mean?

JOE: Do you go away a lot?

SUSANNE: That's my job.

JOE: And what do you write about?

SUSANNE: Health.

JOE: And Beauty? You have a lot to teach.

SUSANNE: *(Beat.)* Thank you. And you? What work do you do?

JOE: Business.

SUSANNE: Oh yes?

JOE: International markets.

SUSANNE: Meaning?

JOE: Trusts. Funds. Stocks.

SUSANNE: That stuff. Loses me.

JOE: I'll help you.

SUSANNE: *(Playing with the words.)* Nikkei. Hang Sen.

JOE: *(Moving closer.)* Footsie. *(Pause.)* You want another drink?

SUSANNE: This Bison is good.

JOE: This man.

SUSANNE: Yes?

JOE: You wait for. How well do you know him?

SUSANNE: How do you know it's a guy? *(JOE points to her outfit.)* I always dress like this.

JOE: That must be dangerous.

SUSANNE: Why?

JOE: *(Slightly tongue in cheek.)* Strange men want to know who you are. *(Beat.)* Who are you?

SUSANNE: You are flirting with me!

JOE: Never! I appreciate a woman who knows how to dress. That's why I hate London and Berlin and I love Paris. Here the boulevards are full of women with style. Even the plain dress nice. I am glad you are not a women's libber.

SUSANNE: How do you know?

JOE: High heels.

SUSANNE: And those women wear?

JOE: Jackboots!

SUSANNE: You're funny.

JOE: You like me?

SUSANNE: I said you're funny.

JOE: How long you going to give your friend?

SUSANNE: Why?

JOE: Well if he doesn't turn up, may I invite you to supper? Unless of course, you don't want to be seen with a guy old enough to be your father!

SUSANNE: My father! That's ridiculous. Anyway I'm not hungry.

JOE: Yet.

SUSANNE: I should wait a half hour in case he shows.

JOE: So that means yes?

SUSANNE: Does it?

JOE: Tell me your name.

SCENE EIGHTEEN

SUSANNE is on the phone to KOBY.

SUSANNE: He's what you said. If I didn't know I'd almost go for him.

We had oysters in Les Deux Magots. No of course not.

We have a kind of picnic date in the Luxembourg Gardens. How do I play it? OK, I'll call. No, of course I am alright.

SOUND EFFECTS IN SCENE CHANGE

(She is changing in front of the audience and this moment is almost-voyeuristic except we do not see the man. He is all the men that try and pick her up every day.)

FRENCH MAN V/O: Hello beauty! Do you speak French? Where are you from? Do you want a drink?

Let me invite you to dinner. Wow you are really something. A smile like that could make a guy kill!

SCENE NINETEEN

PARIS

The Luxembourg Gardens. Paris. Birdsong.

JOE: Thank you.

SUSANNE: For what?

JOE: Agreeing to meet a man who tried to pick you up in a hotel bar. Oh God, I stink of perfume! I was walking through Galeries Lafayette when this woman squirted me with after-shave. In the Metro people moved away from me. I smell like an old whore!

(He dances around to waft it away.)

SUSANNE: *(Laughing.)* You are crazy! You know that? *(Beat.)* But you're not just any man, are you?

JOE: *(Stops.)* What?

SUSANNE: I mean you must be an exceptional one.

JOE: Am I?

SUSANNE: Yes. *(Pause.)* A man of steel. *(Pause.)* A steel liver. That vodka in the hotel bar You nearly killed me.

JOE: Me kill you? Never! *(Takes out a bottle of champagne).* This is harmless. And bubbles make ladies smile! Skol!

SUSANNE: You know Skol?

JOE: I get around.

SUSANNE: Why are all those old men marching around in uniforms and medals?

JOE: May 8. It's the end of the war.

SUSANNE: That was thirty-seven years ago!

JOE: Some people have long memories. *(They drink.)* But soon it's time for dinner. *(Smelling himself.)* If you don't mind eating with an overdose of musk.

SUSANNE: I'm not hungry.

JOE: Make an old man happy!

SUSANNE: Old man! *(Sound of air raid siren.)*

What's that? *(Half in jest.)* Are the Germans coming?

JOE: The French do that once a month. Just testing.

SUSANNE: When I was a teenager, I had a French boyfriend.

JOE: And is it true what they say?

SUSANNE: *(Ignoring this with a smile.)* He told me when God invented the world and he saw that he had given France the most delicious food and the best wine and the most varied landscape in the whole world, and he realised how unfair he had been to the rest of the planet. So, to balance it out what do you think he did?

JOE: What?

SUSANNE: He made the French!

JOE: *(He takes out cheese and bread.)* Your friend.

SUSANNE: What?

JOE: The guy you were waiting for. Did he turn up?

SUSANNE: Oh he's an unreliable toad. He called and told me he met some woman.

JOE: You're not his girlfriend?

SUSANNE: No.

JOE: Apart from your husband, do you have another man in your life?

SUSANNE: Are you always so direct?

JOE: We are a direct people.

SUSANNE: There's nobody.

JOE: Suddenly I am very happy. You can't know how much. Sitting here with you. Me. I don't exist. Just a speck on the earth. But now. Here and now. I am in Paris. Drinking champagne with a woman of exceptional beauty. I have never met a woman like you my whole life. I like you very much.

SUSANNE: You make me feel shy.

JOE: That's charming.

SUSANNE: I don't know what to say to you.

JOE: I'd like to make love to you. *(Silence.)*

SUSANNE: I am leaving now.

JOE: It just came out. I'm sorry, I'm sorry.

SUSANNE: I don't even know you.

JOE: You don't let me.

SUSANNE: That's not true. I agreed to meet you. And I'm working here. I'm not in Paris to pick someone up.

JOE: *Pick someone up*, that sounds so cold. Maybe this is destiny. Kismet.

SUSANNE: You believe in that?

JOE: Let me look at your hand.

SUSANNE: What for?

JOE: I want to examine it.

SUSANNE: Examine?

JOE: I'm a doctor.

SUSANNE: What?

JOE: I qualified back in Beirut.

SUSANNE: What kind of doctor?

JOE: A surgeon. But life led me to another direction.

SUSANNE: Which? *(Beat.)* Let me guess. You're a murderer *(Pause.)*

    You killed ten wives.

JOE: I think that's Bluebeard!

SUSANNE: All those you could've saved as a medic, you did kill them by abandoning them for money.

JOE: Not exactly.

SUSANNE: My father was a doctor.

JOE: I thought he was a journalist.

SUSANNE: What? *(Pause.)*

JOE: You said he was a journalist.

SUSANNE: *(Pause.)* Oh look at that little girl! She's got a yo yo! *(Slightly too loud.)* My father was a journalist later in his life, after he retired.

JOE: What sort?

SUSANNE: Gynae and obstetrics.

JOE: Making babies. That's wonderful. *(He seems to be looking at her breasts.)*

SUSANNE: *(Beat.)* I really ought to go.

JOE: Your heart.

SUSANNE: What?

JOE: It's beating fast. Didn't you ever look at a man's chest when he has no shirt on? You can see the pulse rate going up when he's scared. Are you scared?

SUSANNE: Scared of you.

JOE: Be careful with me. I've known beautiful women who play with men.

SUSANNE: I don't do that. *(Pause.)*

VOICE OVER: *Voice of a woman passing. She is speaking in Polish and flirting SUSANNE looks up.*

JOE: Do you know Polish?

SUSANNE: Was that it? What a pretty woman. *(Beat.)* It's late, I should go.

JOE: Your hand please. *(He takes her hand.)* A long lifeline.

SUSANNE: Really?

JOE: There's a child.

SUSANNE: A child?

JOE: I'm never wrong.

SUSANNE: Aren't you? You're tickling me.

JOE: What a smile!

SUSANNE: Can I have my hand back?

JOE: And wait a minute.

SUSANNE: What?

JOE: This is serious.

SUSANNE: What is?

JOE: I can't say.

SUSANNE: You're worrying me.

JOE: That lifeline.

SUSANNE: An early death?

JOE: *(Pouring more champagne.)* You'll live to a hundred.

SUSANNE: You're humouring me.

JOE: Oh look at this.

SUSANNE: What?

JOE: You've a calcium deficiency.

SUSANNE: How do you know?

JOE: White spots on the nails.

SUSANNE: I hate milk. I'm probably Chinese.

JOE: You need someone to look after you, Mia.

SUSANNE: Do I? *(Beat.)* You have a wife.

JOE: Yes.

SUSANNE: Maybe more?

JOE: Only one.

SUSANNE: And children.

JOE: Four girls.

SUSANNE: So why do you seem lonely?

JOE: All men are. Women have their children. But men... and me, I have to travel a lot. But tomorrow I have seats for the opera. Will you come?

SUSANNE: Are you always alone?

JOE: I see fathers with their little boys and this longing goes through me. I used to fight with my father. Just wrestling. I still miss it. I want to do that for my boy. A man needs a son.

SUSANNE: And a woman?

JOE: She also.

SUSANNE: Your wife can...

JOE: Can't have more children. She's too old. That child on your lifeline.

SUSANNE: That's rubbish!

JOE: Maybe it's our son? *(She shrugs.)*

SUSANNE: So why do you look sad?

JOE: Remembering my father and how he talked of opening a bottle of champagne when we got back our land. He knew the names. Brut! Mumm!

SUSANNE: Who was he?

JOE: Just a man. He drank though it's forbidden. He smoked too much. He was always angry.

SUSANNE: Did you love him?

JOE: What a question! Did you love yours?

SUSANNE: Oh mine!

JOE: So your father was a doctor?

SUSANNE: Yes.

JOE: Like me.

SUSANNE: Like me.

JOE: My father would have liked you.

SUSANNE: What did he do?

JOE: He lived in Paradise. There he grew olive trees. Fat, black ones. Like babies' bodies.

SUSANNE: And?

JOE: And then they come and they tear down our trees. I am sixteen. My mother, my father, my sisters, me. All running. I grow up in a house with white stone and then, the Catastrophe comes and I am in a tent. My mother crying. Where are the fat black olives? Why do European strangers have our trees? Live in our house?

What do we have but dust? *(As if to his father.)* Why do you not fight them? I say to him. Take back our house?

SUSANNE: You're a Palestinian?

JOE: Oh yes

SUSANNE: I thought you were from Lebanon.

JOE: That's where I ended up. Place called Nahr el-Bared.

SUSANNE: What's that?

JOE: Tent city.

SUSANNE: Your father? Where is he?

JOE: He died five years ago. But his heart froze in May 1948. You don't want to hear all this. Let's have more bubbles. I have a croque monsieur for you.

SUSANNE: Sounds rude!

JOE: I love your direct way of talking. Tell me something?

SUSANNE: What?

JOE: How many brothers have you? Where did you go to school? Who was your first boyfriend?

SUSANNE: So many questions!

JOE: Tell me about Sweden.

SUSANNE: It's a magic country full of wild women and trolls!

JOE: I wish my father could have met you.

SUSANNE: Why do you say that?

JOE: You'll laugh at me.

SUSANNE: What?

JOE: I keep thinking of what would have happened if I'd introduced you to him.

SUSANNE: Why?

JOE: As a woman I like.

SUSANNE: That's silly.

JOE: Don't you ever have silly thoughts? I'm tired Mia. Tired of travelling.

SUSANNE: So stay home.

JOE: It's complicated.

SUSANNE: Don't you like your wife?

JOE: Of course I do. *(She holds up her glass. He fills it.)*

SUSANNE: What's the problem then?

JOE: One day I'll tell you.

SUSANNE: Tell me what?

JOE: Why couldn't I have met you when I was young?

SUSANNE: You're not old.

JOE: You are flattering me.

SUSANNE: I never flatter men.

JOE: No, I don't think you do.

SUSANNE: You're bright and healthy. Your body is good.

JOE: For my age.

SUSANNE: Why do people always look at the outside. I hate it. Look under the skin, that's what people should learn.

JOE: Under yours you are still beautiful.

SUSANNE: I don't know what beauty is.

JOE: Yes you do.

SUSANNE: *(Touching his cheek.)* I wish I had met your father too.

SCENE TWENTY

A BOX AT THE OPERA – PARIS .

They are watching Verdi's Nabucco. The orchestra is playing the Va Pensiero. The Chorus of the Hebrew Slaves. SUSANNE's dress has no sleeves.

JOE: Seven long days and no Mia. I missed you.

SUSANNE: *(Ignoring this.)* It's amazing.

JOE: Don't go away without telling me again. Where were you? Did you meet your husband? Or someone else?

SUSANNE: Listen! It's incredible.

JOE: *(Looking at her.)* Not only the music.

SUSANNE: Stop teasing me.

JOE: Listen when the Chorus sings together. They are yearning for freedom. The slaves want to be in their homeland. Oh that wave of longing. And now the harmony. Then back to the single voice.

SUSANNE: Who are they?

JOE: Nabucco's Hebrews.

SUSANNE: What?

JOE: Jews exiled in Babylon.

SUSANNE: I don't understand.

JOE: Because I'm an Arab?

SUSANNE: Yes.

JOE: First the Jews. Now it's us. This song it has become ours. Our land, our soil, our dreams. Palestine. It takes so much blood. We have to sing now. With one voice.

SUSANNE: I hate what happened to your people. The Jews, they don't deserve a country after what they've done. What have they learned from history? Nothing.

JOE: Who are you?

SUSANNE: What?

JOE: Sometimes you talk like a Palestinian woman. *(Sharp.)* Why is that?

SUSANNE: *(Beat.)* What?

JOE: I don't know who you are

SUSANNE: *(Covering her panic.)* I am Miss Nobody. From Sweden.

I come from a place where the sun shines with the moon. In Stockholm the sun is high late at night all through the summer and you never want to sleep. High and there is the sun and the stars and your skin feels light and your clothes feel heavy.

JOE: What are you doing?

SUSANNE: Being here. With you.

JOE: *(Pause.)* I like that. *(Takes her arm.)* Look at this arm. It's taken thousands of years to make you. I wanted to be a Leonardo but I am nobody. But when I sit with you it doesn't feel like that. I look at your hand, your arm and I can be Leonardo for a second. In you I see how beauty works. How pale and smooth.

SUSANNE: People are looking.

JOE: You are shy. It's normal. I like that. I have known many women. But I have never met one like you.

(She lifts her hand to touch his cheek.)

SCENE TWENTY-ONE

SUSANNE is on the phone to MIKAEL.

Pneumonia? Where did you take her? She's too young to learn to swim. I told you that! Is she better? Good. Tell her I'll be home very soon. I know I've hurt you and I'm sorry.

Of course I called about you too. What? What? I don't believe this. You told her what? I'm dead? How dare you? You can't say that. Let her hear my voice, then she'll know that's a lie! *(Shouting.)* Mikael, don't do this! I am here. I am not dead. *(He has hung up. She has her head in her hands. She recovers. She dials a new number. It is KOBY.)*

Shalom. It's Mia. Can you hear me? Yes. Rue Soufflot. Ten minutes. What? Where's he planning to go? Hell. *(Beat.)* Tonight? Of course I'm ready.

(She dials Sweden again.)

Mikael, why did you do that? I am coming home soon. I don't know. The day after tomorrow. I'm not lying. Why did you say that? You have to tell her the truth. Of course I care. Of course she understands. *(She sees JOE.)* I'll call you back.

SCENE TWENTY-TWO

A COFFEE SHOP IN PARIS

JOE arrives and kisses her on both cheeks.

Sound of French voices in a café.

JOE: Did you get coffee?

SUSANNE: Not yet. The waiter is bringing it.

JOE: You were telephoning somebody.

SUSANNE: Yes.

JOE: Who?

SUSANNE: My husband.

JOE: Your husband! How can I be sure it wasn't another man?

SUSANNE: You're jealous!

JOE: You're right.

SUSANNE: That's ridiculous.

JOE: Why?

SUSANNE: You don't own me.

JOE: One day, I may want to.

SUSANNE: I don't like this.

JOE: Oh I think you do.

SUSANNE: What's wrong with you. You're behaving like…

JOE: an Arab.

SUSANNE: a husband.

JOE: If only I were. *(SUSANNE stands up.)*

SUSANNE: I'm going now.

JOE: It gets difficult with a man and you leave? Like with your Swedish husband ?

SUSANNE: You have daughters. A wife.

JOE: And now that matters to you?

SUSANNE: I've never liked it.

JOE: What's wrong with you?

SUSANNE: What?

JOE: Something's not right. I feel it.

SUSANNE: What?

JOE: One minute hot, the next you freeze me out. How can I trust you?

SUSANNE: What? *Garçon! J'attends un crème ici!*

JOE: Stop this!

SUSANNE: OK I'll stop. *(Pause.)* I'll walk out of here and you'll never see me again and then you can go away and forget all about me.

JOE: You run, whenever it gets close between us you're like a terrified bird. *(Beat.)* I'll tell you something

SUSANNE: What?

JOE: About me.

SUSANNE: Yes?

JOE: You know what my life is? It's running, running, always running. I have to sometimes sit in a room for days. In case anyone is watching me. Sometimes I am involved in learning information for my business. I have to learn to see behind my back. One day I will tell you more. It means I am living nowhere. With no one. Ten long years. Always in a different place. Never in the same bed more than a night. You know how tiring it is never speaking your own language? No woman to share all the things I've done. *(Beat.)* I want to be still, Mia. I want to walk in the parks in Paris and the squares in London. I want to sleep quiet. I want to take you to Rome and Pompeii. I want to be a man with a beautiful woman on his arm. I met you three weeks ago and I can't bear someone else looking at you. Even the dogs and the cats come to you to be stroked, you think it's strange I should be any different?

(She stretches her hand out to him light change.)

TWENTY-THREE

A HOTEL ROOM. THE LOUNGE PART.

There is a champagne bottle and two glasses. In the scene change there is stylised movement to show they are making love.

76

TWENTY-FOUR.

Time lapse. Semi-darkness. He is sleeping. She moves away from him. She stares at him. She walks around restlessly. She picks up her bag. She puts it down. This is repeated several times. SUSANNE stands by the window. JOE joins her. There are fireworks outside.

JOE: Thank you, Mia.

SUSANNE: For what?

JOE: Trusting me.

SUSANNE: Why wouldn't I?

JOE: It's a privilege to be with you.

SUSANNE: Stop that!

JOE: I mean it.

SUSANNE: That's silly.

JOE: Let's drink to us.

SUSANNE: I am a lousy drinker.

JOE: Me too.

SUSANNE: To a great lover! *(They clink and drink.)*

JOE: I have a confession.

SUSANNE: Oh?

JOE: I feel guilty.

SUSANNE: Why?

JOE: Being here with you I have had women. It's not that. To be alone with a woman I
feel so much for, that's something else.

SUSANNE: Joe you are a romantic!

JOE: No! I have to tell you about my life.

SUSANNE: Oh?

JOE: Back home. In Lebanon and in Palestine.

SUSANNE: *(Playing with the word.)* Palestine.

JOE: I was a young hot head.

SUSANNE: What does that mean?

JOE: They thought to marry me off young. They said to father sons would cool me down.

SUSANNE: I understand.

JOE: My cousin Leyla.

SUSANNE: Lay-la.

JOE: She was pretty. She had a sweetness to her. And when our child was expected I was happy. My parents, her parents, everybody so excited. He'll be named after my grandfather. And then when the child is a girl we say, it's not important. Soon we will have a son. But the next and the next and the next. Always girls. *Abu el banat.* That's what they call me in our village. The father of girls. And Leyla is too tired to try again. Take a second wife they all tell me. And Leyla will accept this. But I can't live like a peasant. And I can't hurt her even if she pretends she does not mind.

SUSANNE: You are a good man. Here have some bubbles!

JOE: I blamed her and it is not her fault. But inside I am sad. I am old and I have no sons.

(Sound of fireworks outside. SUSANNE gets up.)

SUSANNE: Fireworks! I love it! And it's not even Bastille Day!

JOE: It sounds like guns in the distance.

SUSANNE: Does it? *(He follows.)* Someone is having a party.

Like us. Not enough Veuve Cliquot!

JOE: A merry widow.

SUSANNE: When the husbands die the wives are free!

JOE: And yours? You are phoning him and look at me. I am waiting for you Mia.

SUSANNE: *(Looking out.)* Wow! So much blue!

JOE: When we were organisms living in the ocean all we could see was the blue of the water and the yellow of the sun. That's the colour we loved first.

SUSANNE: Oh you know everything! Oh I am drunk! Look at that. A light show just for us. Woosh! *(She kisses him lightly.)*

JOE: I like it when you do that. Kiss me properly. You haven't done that yet.

SUSANNE: Oh look!

JOE: Have you ever seen a falling star before?

SUSANNE: On my honeymoon in France when the sky was clear.

JOE: When a star falls to earth all the minerals that are inside plummet into the ground and become dust. That stardust is what makes us.

SUSANNE: You are a Sufi. Can you whirl like a dervish?

JOE: How do you know about all that?

SUSANNE: Because I know all about you!

JOE: So you know I want you again. Tu m'allumes. You light me up!

SUSANNE: Then you will have to catch me! *(JOE pours more. She dances around him.)*

JOE: I didn't know you can dance.

SUSANNE: You don't know me.

JOE: I know that I want you. Again and again and again!

SUSANNE: Then you will have to catch me!

JOE: You can never escape.

SUSANNE: That's what you think! *(He grabs her hard and holds her still.)*

JOE: I am your destiny.

SUSANNE: You shock me.

JOE: And you think I can ever be the same? You crawled into my heart. Why did you do that?

SUSANNE: What?

JOE: Why did you talk to me that night in the hotel?

SUSANNE: You came to me!

JOE: But you were there. Waiting.

SUSANNE: Not for you.

JOE: *(Half playful, half anxious.)* It doesn't look that way.

SUSANNE: *(Pause.)* I was working.

JOE: Working? A woman like you should never work.

Why did you come to Paris?

SUSANNE: I don't understand you.

JOE: I was happy. I saw that face and now, my life, it's shattered.

SUSANNE: That's enough.

JOE: Why did you do it?

SUSANNE: I can just walk out.

JOE: No it's for a reason.

SUSANNE: Stop pushing me.

JOE: Please don't say that. Not now.

SUSANNE: Joe!

JOE: Don't you understand. I would leave everything for you, My family. The people I gave my word to. Do you have any idea what I will sacrifice for you?

SUSANNE: I won't let you say this.

JOE: We'll travel. Anywhere you want. Africa. Australia. The end of the earth. I will show you worlds you have never even dreamed.

SUSANNE: I am not listening.

JOE: With you I can have a boy. Or a girl.

SUSANNE: A girl?

JOE: Ours! And I would love her more than my life!

(She shrugs him off violently.)

SUSANNE: You know nothing. Leave me alone. This face! You talk about this face! You know what? I want to slash it! *(She takes a gun from her bag and points it at him. He is shocked. Silence.)*

JOE: They sent you. You want to kill me.

(He opens his arms. He walks towards her. She does not move.)

You already have.

(He turns his back on her and leaves. She breathes hard and remembers her child).

(Yelling.) Ma-le-na!

BLACKOUT.

SCENE TWENTY-FIVE

Sound of Swedish pilot.

VOICE OFF: Ladies and gentlemen. This is your captain speaking. We have now landed at Stockholm Arlanda Airport. We were pleased to serve you on this flight from Paris today and look forward to welcoming you back soon to Swedish Airways.

Sound of plane taxi-ing. It cross fades with birdsong.

SCENE TWENTY-SIX. SWEDEN.

SUSANNE: Look Malena

Look! I've got you a present. Your own canary. Just for you. I'll feed him til you grow bigger and then you can give him seeds and a little lettuce each day. When I was away, in a big city called Paris, I saw a woman. In the Luxembourg Gardens. She had a baby at her breast which all the world could see and the girl she was your age, in a pink dress. And she was too old to take the breast but too young to walk properly. And there she was sucking and the mother, who was wearing a headscarf, not like Brigitte Bardot or Catherine Deneuve but like a Muslim. Just sitting there with her head covered and her breast exposed. And I couldn't stop looking at the mother and the daughter. And it made me think of you and I knew then that I can never leave you. I have come back Malena. We will be together. Mummy and Daddy and our beautiful girl.

(She senses something and turns. There is a man in the shadows.)

Oh!

(To the child.) Look at your bird. Over there! Show mummy how fast you can go!

Look! Run to him. Run quickly! Go! *(The child moves away.)*

It's me you've come for. Don't touch her.

(Sound. Gun shot.)

MALENA (V/O): Mama! *(Sound of the canary singing.)*

BLACKOUT.

END

BROKEN ENGLISH

Broken English is dedicated to the memory of my father, Cecil Fridjohn.

Broken English by Julia Pascal, reading at The Drill Hall on 5 October 2009

Cast:

SOL	Timothy Block
JOSEPH	Jonathan Hansler
HARRY	Paul Herzberg
IRENE	Fiz Marcus
MAX	Marc Pickering

Directed by Julia Pascal

Characters

HARRY BLOOM
44

ISAAC JACOBS known as MAX
22

IRENE GOLD
44

JOSEPH ADLER
30

SOLOMON MONTAGUE
(known as THE PROFESSOR)
55-60

The action happens on 15 January 1947 in a room in a rented flat in London's East End. It is based on a true incident.

Between 1946 and 1948, cells of Jewish activists were raising money for guns to fight the British in Palestine. This was an act of resistance against Foreign Secretary Ernest Bevin's White Paper which limited Jewish entry into Palestine. These British Jews were sympathetic to the violent methods practised by Stern and Irgun Zwai Leumi whose leader was Menachim Begin.

ACT ONE

SCENE ONE

January 15 1947

A large room with a table and several chairs. It's a cluttered bed-sit with old newspapers, clothes and rags all over the place. HARRY is typing a letter and listening to the radio.

RADIO V/O: 'Here is the nine o'clock news from the BBC Home Service.

(He moves the tuner to try and get a better sound and loses it to Mozart.)

Mr. Bevin denounced what he called the murderous terrorists *(Strains from Don Giovanni.)* the British Mandate in Palestine *(Mozart intercuts)* blew up the King David Hotel in Jerusalem last year *(Back to Mozart.)* raided banks in Jaffa and sabotaged police compounds…'

(HARRY sings the Mozart with the radio as he searches among the clutter. He finds his army uniform, puts it on. For a few moments he marks time on the spot. The door opens. MAX enters with a black leather bag. He passes it to HARRY who takes it gingerly and opens it. HARRY takes out a revolver and whistles. He returns it to the bag which he hides under the table)

HARRY: How many?

MAX: Three Stens. Two Enfields.

HARRY: Anyone see you?

MAX: What you take me for? *(HARRY takes off his uniform and gets back into his own clothes.)*

HARRY: You're late. I was anxious.

MAX: No buses. I had to walk

HARRY: *(Beat.)* Did you shave this morning?

MAX: Yeh.

HARRY: Not 'yeh'. 'Yes'

MAX: The fog's so thick, conductor walks in front of his bus with a torch. I get off and I can't even see my own hand in front of me. And it's brass monkey out there. Can't you light that fire?

HARRY: *(He picks up solitary lump of coal and shrugs.)*

MAX: Any tea going?

HARRY: What am I? A nippy in Lyon's Corner?[1] How is she?

MAX: Mrs Gold?

HARRY: Yes.

MAX: Fine.

HARRY: That's all?

MAX: Bit nervous.

HARRY: Nervous. We're all bloody nervous. Was she alone?

MAX: Yeh.

HARRY: Good. *(Silence.)* What's up?

MAX: What?

HARRY: I can smell it. There's something.

MAX: Nothing.

HARRY: Was she careful?

MAX: She's done it before hasn't she?

HARRY: What?

MAX: Hiding stuff.

HARRY: Don't ask questions.

MAX: She asked plenty.

HARRY: Oh?

MAX: About you.

HARRY: And what did you say?

1   He is abbreviating 'Lyon's Corner House,' a popular large restaurant and café. A nippy was a waitress who served there. She was dressed in a maid's cap and apron.

MAX: Schtum.

HARRY: Was her kid there? What's his name?

MAX: Adam. He's away. No one saw nothing.

HARRY: If you say so.

MAX: What you writing?

HARRY: Letter to *The Times*.

MAX: *(Takes the letter and reads.)*

Dear Sir,

Lord Balfour promised Palestine to the Jews as a homeland. We Jews fought and died in the British Army fighting fascism and how are we rewarded? With the Foreign Secretary waving The White Paper, in our faces. And what does it say? "No more Jews in Palestine".

(HARRY takes the letter and rips it up.)

HARRY: Waste of time.

MAX: Dresden. Berlin. Hanover. All those bombs. *(Beat.)* Why not the railway?

HARRY: What you on about?

MAX: It really bothers me you know that.

HARRY: What?

MAX: Auschwitz.

HARRY: Oh that

MAX: Why didn't we bomb it?

HARRY: Because 'we', that is Churchill, didn't want to risk English pilots/

MAX: They knew all about it. Back in 43/

HARRY: /just to save the Yids

MAX: /a few bombs on those tracks and think how many lives

HARRY: *(Interrupts.)* would have been banging on the doors to get to Palestine?

MAX: When did you get involved with all this?

HARRY: Wouldn't you like to know!.

MAX: You want to go there?

HARRY: Where?

MAX: Palestine.

HARRY: Don't you?

MAX: I want to see Jaffa. Haifa. Tel Aviv. Jerusalem.

HARRY: Where it stinks of God?

MAX: What does that mean?

HARRY: I want a state but I don't want all that religious guff.

MAX: Who do you support? Menachim Begin?

HARRY: The Pole? I don't care about names. I just want
    the Brits out *(Picking up ripped pieces of paper.)* Maybe I
    should've sent this.

MAX: No.

HARRY: Why not?

MAX: If they check up on you…

HARRY: Paranoid. *(Beat.)* Irene Gold

MAX: What about her?

HARRY: Something's up.

MAX: No it's not.

HARRY: You said she was asking questions?

MAX: She sends her love.

HARRY: What?

MAX: Or was it regards?

HARRY: You look guilty.

MAX: Me?

HARRY: You and her?

MAX: What about it?

HARRY: Something happen?

MAX: Any tea going?

HARRY: Later.

MAX: Dry as a wooden crate.

HARRY: What?

MAX: Never mind.

HARRY: Why a wooden crate?

MAX: Shall I boil some hot water then?

HARRY: Wait til the others get here. I don't want you
schlepping all over the house.

MAX: How long you got this place?

HARRY: A few months

MAX: What happened to your manor?

HARRY: Hilda's there.

MAX: Kick you out did she? *(Silence.)*

HARRY: *(Shivers.)* You're right. It is brass monkey. *(He puts on
an old cardigan.)* I could do with a real drink. Warm me up.
When did I last have a decent Scotch. *(Beat.)* … You didn't
finish.

MAX: What?

HARRY: Irene Gold.

MAX: Oh her.

HARRY: Well? What was she asking?

MAX: I had to…

HARRY: What?

MAX: You know…

HARRY: Do I?

MAX: She was jumpy about the stuff

HARRY: What?

MAX: I had to 'calm her down'.

HARRY: You shtupped her. Is that what you're telling me?

MAX: What?

HARRY: You heard.

MAX: I don't like that word.

HARRY: Since when did you get refined?

MAX: We shouldn't speak Yiddish.

HARRY: So you shtupped Irene Gold. Well, well.

MAX: Forget it.

HARRY: Forget it? Markie comes home and finds you and his missis and you say forget it!

MAX: He's up north. Selling menswear

HARRY: Me and Markie. We were comrades. In the Party. You don't shtup a comrade's wife.

MAX: Men's suits. All colours. Charcoal. Pigeon grey. He's gone to Manchester. Or is it Leeds? Summer it's Indian cotton. Now he's carrying winter lines. Wool mix. And some new fibre. From America.

HARRY: I don't care if he's selling suits made from barbed wire. Do you know what you're doing when you shtup someone in the organisation?

MAX: Relax will you.

HARRY: You're finished.

MAX: I said relax.

HARRY: Yes. Relax. That's just what I'm going to do. *(Beat.)* How's Nina?

MAX: How should she be?

HARRY: I don't know. I'm being polite. I ask after your mother.

You don't like me to use words like 'shtupping', so now I'm being polite. Is that alright?

MAX: She's fine. My mother's fine. *(HARRY starts sparring with MAX.)*

HARRY: Come on! Come on! What shape are you in?

MAX: Not now. I know your right hook.

HARRY: Show me some action!

MAX: OK daddio.

HARRY: My kid'd be smarter than you. Better looking than you. Taller than you.

MAX: You don't have a kid. *(They spar for a while then HARRY, vaudeville-style, makes out that MAX has hit him and does a prat fall.)*

HARRY: And the winner is *(He lifts MAX's arm.)*

MAX: You don't have to tell me. I know I'm rubbish.

HARRY: What's up?

MAX: I've had nothing to eat all day.

HARRY: Worked up an appetite with Irene did you? *(Pause.)* Your mother and I. We were neighbours you know.

MAX: Yeh?

HARRY: When you were born. Nina was very worried about her little Isaac.

MAX: Don't call me that.

HARRY: Too Jewish is it?

MAX: I prefer Max.

HARRY: She liked the name Isaac. The sacrificed son.

MAX: I thought Isaac was saved at the last minute.

HARRY: Just testing.

MAX: You think I'm thick, don't you.

HARRY: Who was his brother?

MAX: What you on about?

HARRY: Well half brother.

MAX: Who?

HARRY: Isaac's.

MAX: How should I know?

HARRY: It's your heritage, you nebbish. You should be curious, about everything. Even the Bible.

MAX: Opium of the masses.

HARRY: Abraham's first son. Sent out to the desert.

MAX: That's the Arab story. *(Beat.)* And what do we do about them.

HARRY: We'll worry about that later. *(Beat.)* Ishmael.

MAX: What?

HARRY: Isaac's brother. *(Beat.)* Same father. Different mother. You never had a brother did you?

MAX: What you on about?

HARRY: Your mother. Snappy dresser. All the boys wanted Nina.

MAX: Yeh well now she's fat.

HARRY: Fat is she?

MAX: You and her?

HARRY: What about it?

MAX: You do her?

HARRY: *(Beat.)* I don't remember.

MAX: There were that many?

HARRY: I was young.

MAX: And you have a go at me!

HARRY: I was a lad.

MAX: So I hear. You had them all. Jews. Shicksas.

HARRY: I'm an internationalist. *(Beat.)* Did I have your mother? No I don't think so. I'd've remembered. *(Beat.)* Very fat?

MAX: What you on about her for?

HARRY: Would you say she is obese? Nice word that. Oh-bees. Is it Latin?

MAX: Give it up will you.

HARRY: *(Beat.)* And Irene?

MAX: What about her?

HARRY: Obese too is she?

MAX: I thought you'd seen her.

HARRY: We lost touch.

MAX: How's that?

HARRY: The war.

MAX: So how's she involved?

HARRY: She's reliable. Everyone knows that. I remember Irene Gold when she was Irene Levy. Used to be friends with your mother. Used to be quite something that Irene.

MAX: Yeh?

HARRY: Real looker.

MAX: She's not bad for her age.

HARRY: You going to shtup her again?

MAX: Course not.

HARRY: That means yes *(Pause.)*

MAX: You used to fancy Irene?

HARRY: You said she's obese.

MAX: Who else is coming here?

HARRY: You'll see.

MAX: Must be serious.

HARRY: I hate this hanging around. Suppose the others get picked up?

MAX: You're too jumpy.

HARRY: Lucky you weren't arrested. Looking like that. You've got to be smart on the street. You? You look like drek. *(Beat.)* Tell me. You and Irene, how many times?

MAX: You're jealous!

HARRY: Look at you. You're all stubble.

MAX: Didn't want to use Markie's razor.

HARRY: Why not?

MAX: Didn't seem decent.

HARRY: You can shtup his wife but you can't use his razor?

MAX: OK. OK.

HARRY: Lobos!

MAX: I said OK. Next time I'll take my own blade.

HARRY: There'll be no next time. Leave your schmuck in your pants can't you.

MAX: I'll make some tea.

HARRY: No going out on the landing.

MAX: I need something hot.

HARRY: You'll wait.

MAX: Got to get warm. I only had a cuppa. Brick Lane.

HARRY: Assam or Darjeeling?

MAX: In the cuff, there was a kid. Seventeen maybe. Purple spots all over his face. Ready to burst. Army uniform. He was reading *The Daily Worker*. I got talking to him.

HARRY: What?

MAX: I'm saying. You poor sod, you're going to Palestine and in my bag here's the gun that will kill you'. *(HARRY hits MAX in the gut.)*

HARRY: You stupid schmuck. You don't even think it. You hear?

MAX: In my head, that's where I'm saying it. Shit. Where you learn to hit like that?

HARRY: I was thumping Mosley's men when you were pissing your gatkes.

MAX: Fucking fuck you. I should've seen that coming.

HARRY: If you're serious about being with us, you've got to anticipate at all times. You don't relax. Ever. You want out?

MAX: Why would I?

HARRY: You should consider. *(Looking in MAX's pockets.)* And what's this?

MAX: Chopped liver.

HARRY: Present from Irene Gold I suppose.

MAX: For my dinner.

HARRY: She does the business and then makes you sandwiches. *(Eats.)* You must be quite a goer. Like you does she?

MAX: She didn't complain. Leave me a bit will you?

HARRY: They say a man shtups like his father. Some kind of inherited memory. You think that's true? Now if a father and son shtup the same woman then she could answer that couldn't she. *(Beat.)* For God's sake where's Sol? *(Beat.)* Get up man. Look at Maxie. A regular little Hercules.

MAX: Size isn't everything. You eating all that?

HARRY: *(Gives him half the sandwich.)* Does she know she gave birth to a warrior? Your mother? A David. A Spartacus. A Judah Maccabee? She must have been proud of you. That Nina. Is she? Is she proud? And Johnny? Proud of his son is he? Is he?

(Knocking at the door.)

MAX: *(Getting up fast.)* Who's that?

HARRY: The landlady.

V/O: I know you're in there. You can't hide from me.

MAX: What?

HARRY: Shut it!

V/O: Mr Bloom. I'm asking you for the three months' rent. I'll give you until tomorrow morning. You want me to call the police? *(Silence.)*

MAX: She's gone.

HARRY: Second time today.

MAX: She heard us.

HARRY: She's deaf. *(He turns on the radio. Elgar's Nimrod.)*

MAX: Short of spondulux old man?

HARRY: *(Mock posh.)* Not much call for a hansom cabriolet these days

MAX: You should drive around Buck House. Get some fares from our German king and his fat wife.

HARRY: You should go home now.

MAX: What?

HARRY: You've done the job. Get an early night.

MAX: But what about the meeting?

HARRY: Some shut eye.

MAX: Trying to get rid of me Harry?

HARRY: Could get dirty. Not good for your health

MAX: And what does that mean?

HARRY: Heart isn't it?

MAX: Rubbish.

HARRY: Any more chopped liver?

MAX: *(Reaches in his pocket.)* Try this.

HARRY: Herring. Not bad. Just like the wife never made.

MAX: Where is Mrs Bloom?

HARRY: She's very good that Irene Gold. At sandwiches. Could do with more pickle. Not sure you're cut out for all this.

MAX: Left you has she?

HARRY: Bit more gherkin…

MAX: Hilda?

HARRY: *(Turns off the radio.)* Yes?

MAX: Catch you on the nest did she?

HARRY: I'm a good boy.

MAX: Why no kids?

HARRY: What?

MAX: You never mention…

HARRY: No!

MAX: No boy chicks?

HARRY: Infertile. Sterile. Barren.

MAX: You?

HARRY: Her. *(Shrugs.)* Me.

MAX: *(Beat.)* Sorry

HARRY: You got the right idea.

MAX: What's that?

HARRY: Shtupping other people's wives. *(Beat.)* And they give you lunch. You must be knackered.

MAX: I'm alright.

HARRY: This stuff's not for you.

MAX: What?

HARRY: The heavy stuff.

MAX: What's all this about?

HARRY: You see I don't think you're really up to it.

MAX: I don't believe this. Is this about Irene Gold?

HARRY: Well you've done the transportation but I'd say, you're not yet ready for the real action.

MAX: Who says?

HARRY: I do.

MAX: And you decide. What about Sol?

HARRY: He takes my advice.

MAX: Does he now? *(JOSEPH appears at the door.)*

JOSEPH: Shalom chaver!

HARRY: For God's sake who let you in?

JOSEPH: I waited til your landlady went to the King's Arms.
I'd say she's a Guinness drinker. Bet you sixpence.

HARRY: Did she see you?

JOSEPH: Not a chance!

HARRY: How do you know?

JOSEPH: Nobody sees me.

HARRY: What?

JOSEPH: I'm transparent. *(Beat.)* And you?

HARRY: Max Jacobs.

JOSEPH: Joseph Adler.

MAX: Shalom.

HARRY: You're late.

JOSEPH: The gear. Here is it?

MAX: Yes.

HARRY: Keep your voices down!

JOSEPH: Sorry.

HARRY: It's safe.

JOSEPH: Where?

HARRY: Don't you worry. *(JOSEPH picks up a newspaper.)*

JOSEPH: Why do you hoard all this junk? Look at this. Falling
apart. January the thirtieth nineteen hundred and thirty-
three.

MAX: Fourteen years you keep a newspaper?

JOSEPH: *(Reading.)* Adolf Hitler elected Reichschancellor of
Germany.

MAX: Yeh.

HARRY: It's 'yes' how many times. *(Beat.)* Our young Max.
Quite a hero. Going to take on the British army. Clear
them out of Palestine all by himself. Look our boy. A
Lenin. A Stalin. A reader of Das Kapital. Auf Deutsch!

MAX: Bugger off. *(The radio plays dance band music from the 1930s.)*

JOSEPH: Will you listen to that. Real Café de Paris here. *(Takes a chair and waltzes with it. He talks to the chair as if it were a woman.)* Will you stop treading on my metatarsals. You'll do me damage and no woman will look at me after you're done... Will you look at her. Feet like a navvy and the knees of a crustacean. My ma warned me about women like you. Only after one thing. Me medical books

(HARRY switches the radio off. JOSEPH puts chair down. He's miffed. He looks around the room.) Quite a museum here. You should chuck it out. *(He turns the radio back on but at a lower level.)* Why's The Professor called us altogether?

HARRY: Something's up.

JOSEPH: He should've been here half an hour ago. He's never late.

MAX: You Irish?

JOSEPH: *Tir na nog.* From the land of the beautiful and the young. Before I was Irish I was Welsh. Kaunus to Cardiff and Cardiff to/

MAX: Cork?

JOSEPH: /Dublin. At school they beat my head in for talking like a Welshman. So I learnt to talk like this. To keep the little brain I've got. *(JOSEPH yawns.)* Sorry gentlemen. Don't know what's wrong with me. Can't stop yawning.

HARRY: Joseph's a doctor. Royal London.

MAX: I wanted to be a medic. Or a lawyer. Someone they'd look up to. All I'm good for is making rubbish furniture in a freezing shed down the Kingsland Road.

HARRY: Furniture-maker my arse. He runs around moving people's stuff in a broken -down van. He should get into the fur trade. I tell him. What does he earn? Two pounds a week when he could be getting an extra half a sheet.

MAX: Yesterday. I get this man coming round. Clear the warehouse he says. Just a few tables. I drives there in the van in that bleeding fog, takes me hours and it's not a few tables, it's a huge load full of fucking huge office cabinets. I have to schlep the buggers out in my van and take them to the dump. And on the way I think well maybe I can sell the bastards. Make half a sheet. So I drives them round to this geezer I know who buys and sells stuff and I says, make me an offer. And he says, no go mate. This lot's all oak and the fashion now, it's teak. And at the end of the day I'm stuck with twenty two stinking oak cabinets that nobody wants and not a pot to piddle in. Fucking teak. I ask you.

JOSEPH: Better than being a shit doctor. Every night I wake up sweating. I'm re-sitting. Greek. Latin. Can't remember a bloody word. Is there tea made?

MAX: So why do it?

JOSEPH: Ma didn't want me to end up like my da. Selling pictures of the Holy Virgin to the Catholics.

MAX: I like that.

JOSEPH: Oh sure it's bloody poetic.

MAX: It's a laugh.

JOSEPH: The Jewman and his boy schlepping all over County Dublin, County Wicklow, County Cork. My da. Disappearing with Kathleen or Siobhan. He comes back to Dolphin's Barn Road. Strange smell on his fingers. *(Beat.)* Did you say there was char?

HARRY: I'll make.

JOSEPH: Years later. I recognise it.

MAX: Oh yeh?

JOSEPH: My hand up some nurse's skirt. It was woman. *(Takes off his jacket off.)* Hot in here. You got the gas on?

HARRY: And pay with what?

MAX: You want some herring? *(He offers a sandwich.)*

JOSEPH: What I really want is something sweet. Barley sugar or chocolate. Don't suppose, no, this will do fine. *(JOSEPH eats.)* Ma usually sends a fowl from Dublin.

HARRY: Can't remember the last time I ate chicken. *(He leaves.)*

JOSEPH: But this week there's bugger all in the post. Some bloody arse of a postman's nicked my hen. *(Beat.)* Ata Midaber Ivrit? Speak Hebrew?

MAX: What for?

JOSEPH: Are are you still circumcised? Or did it grow back when you read Karl Marx?

MAX: What do you know.

JOSEPH: I know you'll need Hebrew not Russian in the new state. Why have you never learned?

MAX: I had other things to do.

JOSEPH: Zaide taught me.

MAX: Your grandfather!

JOSEPH: Aleph, bet, gimmel, dalet, hey and if I didn't get it quick I've his strap on my arse.

MAX: I like it better when you're talking about women.

JOSEPH: And if I did well there's a farthing a lesson. I'm twelve years old and I've got empty milk bottles full of brass lined up on the windowsill. Every night I'm dreaming of the bike I'll get for my barmitzvah with this spondulux. I'm running downstairs at first light on my thirteenth birthday and the sill's empty. Where's my money? They've only gone and taken it for my sister's dowry. Load of shite. *(Silence.)*

MAX: How you know Harry?

JOSEPH: *(Shouting out to HARRY mock posh.)* Now was it Eton or Harrow? Or was it with the Professor at Cambridge. Not sure I can remember can you Harold? *(HARRY arrives with the tea.)*

HARRY: *(Mock posh.)* Tea gentlemen? *(Joseph goes for the tea.)*

JOSEPH: I don't mind if I do. *(Back to normal.)* When I was in India in 42, I saw an old man, very thin, sitting in the dirt drinking tea. He had a worm growing out of his nose.

HARRY: Eat it did you?

JOSEPH: And the nurses out in India. Lovely. Real women. And they'd spend the night with you for a few rupees. *(JOSEPH sings over the next few lines.)*

JOSEPH: *I've got sixpence. Jolly jolly sixpence/*

MAX: *(Puts his sandwich down)* And you, where were you?

JOSEPH: */I've got sixpence/*

HARRY: *(Beat.)* Isle of Man.

JOSEPH: */to last me all my life/*

MAX: You interned?

JOSEPH: */I've got tuppence to lend/*

HARRY: Well I wasn't on holiday.

JOSEPH: */And tuppence to spend/*

HARRY: Got a British passport yet?

JOSEPH: */and tuppence to get myself a wife.*

HARRY: You want to see it?

JOSEPH: *(Showing his.)* Look. Captain Joseph Adler. Look at that! Two years in India serving His Majesty while my cousins get the privilege of digging their own grave before Jerry puts a bullet through their heads. Captain that's me. Not bad for a stinking Jewish Welsh Irishman. Maybe I should have married an Indian girl. Brought her back here. Poor buggers with the British lording it over them. But bye bye Tommy, India'll soon be free.

HARRY: What about the Muslims?

JOSEPH: What about them?

JOSEPH: Get the British out. Hindus and Muslims live together like brothers.

HARRY: Like us and the Arabs.

JOSEPH: Why not? If we get a state. When. Will you live there?

MAX: What? In the desert?

HARRY: You can make it bloom. Or sell that teak!

JOSEPH: But you know even if we hate this place, we're alright here.

MAX: How do you reckon?

JOSEPH: Well the English didn't put us in gas ovens did they.

MAX: Well that was 'jolly decent' of them. *(Beat.)* And why, exactly don't they let us in to their precious Mandate? Tell me that.

HARRY: *(Mock posh.)* More tea gentlemen? Oh golly gosh, I am clean out of milk and sugar,

JOSEPH: Any lemon?

HARRY: What about cucumber sandwiches?

JOSEPH: Does it cost to ask? A lemon tea would be grand.

HARRY: Those Itis. They were always going on about Amalfi lemons. I haven't seen a lemon since before the war.

JOSEPH: Her name was Rahila.

MAX: Whose?

JOSEPH: The Indian nurse. Breasts like little apples.

MAX: I like little titties not like great cow's udders.

HARRY: How much longer til The Professor gets here? I hate this stuff sitting around.

JOSEPH: I'm not sure I trust him.

HARRY: What?

JOSEPH: All that English gent stuff. I don't like it. Sounds like his mother sent him to elocution.

HARRY: She did.

JOSEPH: All that Cambridge bull.

HARRY: It's perfect cover.

MAX: So what's this meeting for?

JOSEPH: He's late. Got himself picked up. Maybe we should all leave now. *(He straightens the chairs.)*

HARRY: You scared?

JOSEPH: What?

HARRY: You are. I can feel it.

JOSEPH: Why am I sweating? *(Smells his armpits.)* Lamb chops. I stink of lamb chops. If only I could eat myself. With mint sauce. Wish I could stop this yawning. This brain, this grey fat, it's only a tool. Make it think about something else! Something to be proud of. It's coming. A state for Jews. Jewish policemen. Jewish street cleaners. Jewish farmers. Jewish soldiers. *(Takes out a small notebook.)* The 'historical imperative'. I learnt that expression yesterday. A shrinking vocabulary is like a tumour. It just moves silently through your whole body. You don't realise til it's too late. *(Beat.)* Pity there's no cake with this tea. Or even a dry biscuit. *(He straightens the chairs.)* Did you know there is a 97 million to one chance that you are you? That's how many sperms fight to get to the egg and only one gets through. *(Pause.)* What's that?

HARRY: What?

JOSEPH: Someone on the landing.

MAX: I can't hear anything.

JOSEPH: The landlady.

HARRY: You said she was out

JOSEPH: I saw her.

HARRY: Well then she's back. For the rent. Can you spare a fiver? *(Gentle tapping at the door.)* It's not her.

MAX: Maybe it's 'him'?

HARRY: He's got the key.

JOSEPH: Open the door.

HARRY: *(Loud whisper.)* No! *(Woman's voice offstage.)*

IRENE: It's Irene! *(HARRY opens it. IRENE stands there in coat, a hat and with a black silk scarf around her neck. Pause.)*

IRENE: Harry.

HARRY: Hello Irene.

IRENE: It's freezing out there. Aren't you going to invite me in?

HARRY: You should put more clothes on.

IRENE: Coldest winter in living memory. Hello Joseph. I didn't expect to see you here.

JOSEPH: Well, well. Mrs Gold.

IRENE: A long time.

JOSEPH: I remember you. Irene Levy, the tailor's daughter from the Commercial Road. We used to go hiking, Habonim. Or was it Maccabi? I was twenty. Over from Dublin. You were a young girl then. You still are

MAX: Why you here Irene?

IRENE: I just wanted to know that everything's alright

HARRY: Why shouldn't it be?

JOSEPH: Is she involved?

HARRY: Don't ask.

MAX: *(To Irene.)* Did you follow me?

IRENE: I was worried.

MAX: What about?

IRENE: You might get stopped on the way.

HARRY: And how is Mister Gold?

JOSEPH: Her. Here. The Professor'll go loco.

HARRY: How you get this address? *(To Max.)* You tell her?

MAX: What you take me for?

HARRY: It's not safe here.

IRENE: I don't care.

HARRY: I'm not talking about you.

IRENE: Oh.

HARRY: You put us all at risk, did you think of that, did you?

MAX: You did, didn't you/

IRENE: /What?

MAX: /follow me?

IRENE: I wanted to see Harry

JOSEPH: Well now you've seen him go home Missis.

HARRY: Me? Why?

MAX: What do you want with him?

IRENE: It's been a long time Harry. You've gone grey.

HARRY: You haven't.

JOSEPH: When he finds her here, what will he say?

IRENE: Can't I be useful?

JOSEPH: How do you mean?

IRENE: I don't know. What do women do? Type letters. Make
    tea.

JOSEPH: No tea. No typewriter here.

HARRY: You kept your looks. *(Silence.)*

JOSEPH: The Professor…

HARRY: What?

JOSEPH: …he won't like it.

IRENE: I'll leave.

JOSEPH: *(Mock posh.)* If you'll excuse us.

HARRY: She stays.

JOSEPH: Your funeral.

HARRY: Bring any herring?

IRENE: Herring?

HARRY: I remember when I used to come round to yours with Hilda. Very good schmaltz herring. Lots of imagination with your herring. Dill, olive oil, lemon, kaez un smetna.

IRENE: You've a good memory. *(Pause.)*

HARRY: And the piano?

IRENE: What about it?

HARRY: You were something!

IRENE: Not really.

HARRY: Irene played for the silent films. I used to watch her.

JOSEPH: Is that so?

HARRY: Me and Irene. Concerts. Royal Albert Hall. Myra Hess. Beethoven. Chopin.

MAX: *(Sarcastic.)* How nice!

HARRY: Still go?

IRENE: Markie is tone deaf.

JOSEPH: Who roped you in to all this?

HARRY: Oh she's the original. Irene was in love with Palestine when I was dreaming of Moscow

JOSEPH: Were you in the Party?

IRENE: Wasn't everybody?

JOSEPH: And?

IRENE: Stalin gave Hitler half of Poland. How could I be a Communist after that?

MAX: What about you? Irish Republican was it?

JOSEPH: *(Admiringly.)* Ah those boyos!

IRENE: I left the Party. Markie stayed.

MAX: This tea's getting cold. You want some Irene?

JOSEPH: Did you see that?

HARRY: What?

JOSEPH: Lightning!

IRENE: There's nothing.

JOSEPH: There are two Irenes.

MAX: What you on about?

JOSEPH: And you. Your face is breaking up. I need to lie down.

IRENE: I'll help. *(Clears piles of papers off the sofa.)*

MAX: You having a stroke mate? *(He offers a cigarette to Harry.)*

JOSEPH: Migraine.

HARRY: Where do you get that?

MAX: Swapped it for butter. You want it. Or you Irene?

HARRY: *(Taking it.)* Ladies don't. *(He's about to light it.)*

JOSEPH: No. No. Smoke makes it worse. *(HARRY puts the cigarette away for later.)*

MAX: Shall I call a doctor?

HARRY: He is a doctor.

JOSEPH: It'll pass.

HARRY: How long?

JOSEPH: I don't know. Twelve hours.

HARRY: That long! The Professor's on his way. *(JOSEPH takes a rag, puts it over his eyes, lies down, gets up.)*

JOSEPH: I'm going to vomit.

HARRY: The khazi's in the yard. Don't let the landlady see. *(JOSEPH leaves. HARRY turns up the radio to give them more privacy.)*

HARRY: How are you Irene?

IRENE: Fine. I'm fine.

HARRY: You look well. Blooming I'd say. Joseph's right. You've hardly changed since you were a young girl. Blooming. Wouldn't you say she's blooming Max? Get a cup. Brew the lady some Darjeeling. Or maybe I've got some Ceylon? Don't stand there like a klutz. *(MAX goes out on the landing. A waltz plays softly.)*

IRENE: It's been a long time.

HARRY: Eight years.

IRENE: You disappeared.

HARRY: I was picked up.

IRENE: What?

HARRY: Enemy alien.

IRENE: Why did nobody tell me? 'Enemy alien'? You were born here like me.

HARRY: Your parents were born in Whitechapel.

IRENE: Didn't they naturalise?

HARRY: No geld for the papers.

IRENE: Oh.

HARRY: The old man and me. Romanian nationals. Arrested. Like thieves. First they called us filthy Fascists. Then they called us filthy Jews.

IRENE: Why didn't you get in touch?

HARRY: When?

IRENE: I don't know. When you were released? Or in 45?

HARRY: Hilda was a jealous woman.

IRENE: You told her about us?

HARRY: Of course.

IRENE: But we were finished before she began. I hoped we could be friends.

HARRY: Just a friend?

IRENE: What else could we be?

HARRY: Not sure I can be just friends with a woman. *(Beat.)* I shouldn't have sent Max. He's too young for all this.

IRENE: Why did you?

HARRY: Sidney wasn't available *(Silence.)* I heard you were a nurse

IRENE: I drove an ambulance. I miss that. Stuck at home. I could be useful now. I could move the stuff to the next contact. Nobody would suspect a woman.

HARRY: Forget it.

IRENE: Joseph moves it. You move it. Max moves it. Why can't I?

HARRY: There are rules.

IRENE: In Palestine the women do the same as the men…

HARRY: It's war there.

IRENE: And here? *(Pause.)* How do you get the equipment to our boys?

HARRY: Like Hannibal and his elephants. Over the Alps.

IRENE: You don't trust me?

HARRY: Your timing's not great.

IRENE: Next time I'll telephone for an appointment.

HARRY: Tonight we've got a special meeting.

IRENE: I'm in this now as much as you.

HARRY: The less you know/

IRENE: /Don't I have a right/

HARRY: Don't go there!

IRENE: / to know the whole story?

HARRY: Nobody knows that.

IRENE: Somebody must.

HARRY: Not even the Professor.

IRENE: Who's the top brass? *(HARRY shrugs.)* Where do the rifles come from?

HARRY: Please Irene.

IRENE: You ask me to hide the guns that send the English to hell and I can't ask? *(Beat.)* Well?

HARRY: He'll be here soon.

IRENE: How long have you known me?

HARRY: Don't start.

IRENE: We were thirteen.

HARRY: It's safer. Know nothing!

IRENE: But I do know don't I. I know what comes in a bag, gets hidden in my house and is taken away the next day. Does our time together mean nothing to you? *(Sound of the waltz can be heard from the radio. Silence.)*

IRENE: Do you still dance?

HARRY: What?

IRENE: Wednesday nights. Arthur Murray. You and me.

HARRY: Nobody has time to dance now. *(She goes to him they waltz. He breaks away.)*

HARRY: Why haven't you got old or fat? You're supposed to be obese.

IRENE: Tell me Harry. What's going on?

HARRY: I can't.

IRENE: You want to.

HARRY: If you get picked up they'll beat it out of you. You think His Majesty's Government will make exceptions for a 'lady'? This is war Irene.

IRENE: The weapons. Where do they come from? *(She goes up very close to him and kisses him. He responds.)*

IRENE: Don't shut me out.

HARRY: Army issue. Some of our brothers. In the barracks. 'Lost' them.

IRENE: English guns to kill the English.

HARRY: Poetic irony.

IRENE: And how do you get them out of the country?

HARRY: The French gendarmes give our lads a police escort to Marseilles. Three days later our boys are shifting them off the boats in Jaffa *(HARRY whistles the Marseillaise.)*

HARRY: Satisfied? *(Beat.)* And now you should leave.

IRENE: Why?

HARRY: It's the first time he's called us all together.

IRENE: Meaning?

HARRY: Something's up.

IRENE: Something major?

HARRY: Yes.

IRENE: On home ground?

HARRY: That's all I can say.

IRENE: Tell me.

HARRY: I can't.

IRENE: Yes.

HARRY: Go home.

IRENE: Why you so keen to get me out?

HARRY: Let's say I have an interest in your health.

IRENE: Were you thinking about that the first time you sent Sidney round with the guns?

HARRY: Drop it will you.

IRENE: Like you dropped me for Hilda?

HARRY: I made a mistake. You think I don't know that?

IRENE: A mistake? Is that what you think now?

HARRY: I don't know what I think. I see you, I'm all mixed up.

HARRY: You happy with Markie?

IRENE: Why do you ask?

HARRY: Curiosity.

IRENE: That's all?

HARRY: Let's say, over the years…

IRENE: Yes?

HARRY: …I wondered

IRENE: What?

HARRY: If you'd stay with him.

IRENE: What are you saying?

HARRY: I don't know.

IRENE: And you?

HARRY: What?

IRENE: With Hilda?

HARRY: Hilda?

IRENE: Yes.

HARRY: *(Beat.)* Right.

IRENE: Right. *(Pause.)*

HARRY: Look about Hilda. I learned to live with my mistake. There were bigger things than women.

IRENE: Exactly. Do you live here now?

HARRY: This is my 'Head Quarters'. Hilda's in the house.

IRENE: Right. You and her…

HARRY: Hard night?

IRENE: What?

HARRY: You look all in. Max and you. You and Max. That's why you came isn't it. To see Max.

IRENE: See Max? I've just seen Max.

HARRY: So I hear?

IRENE: What does that mean?

HARRY: Needs a good thrashing. Messing with other men's wives. I never touched you after you and Markie got together. Did I?

IRENE: No.

HARRY: I kept away because he was my friend. And God knows it was hard. I stood outside your house. Watching you walk down the street. I wanted to stop you. Take you in my arms and start again because with you it was so deep.

IRENE: You never said.

HARRY: You and me. Kept coming back to me when I was with Hilda.

IRENE: Why didn't you tell me?

HARRY: Your smell. Inside me. Like now. Kept telling myself Harry, Markie's your friend. You can't look him in the eye if you start all that again. Your friend's wife. Some rules. Am I right?

IRENE: I wish I'd known.

HARRY: And what would you have done? Left Markie? Two broken marriages? Divorce?

IRENE: We're not Catholics.

HARRY: But you've got a kid?

IRENE: I can't leave my son.

HARRY: No.

IRENE: If you had a son… *(Silence.)* Does Max know about you and his mother?

HARRY: It was a long time ago. Before you and me.

IRENE: Why did you and Nina break up?

HARRY: She got pregnant. Lost interest.

IRENE: And the father?

HARRY: Not guilty!

IRENE: How do you know?

HARRY: I can't make babies.

IRENE: Maybe not with Hilda.

HARRY: Not with anyone.

IRENE: Are you sure?

HARRY: Don't be ridiculous. Max is Johnny's.

IRENE: Is he?

HARRY: She'd've said. Wouldn't she?

IRENE: Would she?

HARRY: What?

IRENE: Did you never think Max might be your son?

HARRY: What? Doesn't even look like me.

IRENE: Doesn't he?

HARRY: You're just making this up.

IRENE: Why would I?

HARRY: Imagination. Like your piano playing. You go off into another world.

IRENE: And I've known father and son. *(Laughs.)* It's funny your son came out of your schlang and his went into me.

HARRY: Stop this. Stop this right now. I forbid this talk.

IRENE: You forbid it!

HARRY: And you and him? What the hell were you thinking?

IRENE: I'm not your wife.

HARRY: Pity. *(Beat.)* I've made so many royal balls up with women. What about your son. How is Adam?

IRENE: What about him?

HARRY: Is he Markie's?

IRENE: Yes.

HARRY: You sure?

IRENE: There has been only Markie. And you.

HARRY: Aren't you forgetting last night?

IRENE: Except Max. Look Harry I came for a reason.

HARRY: To see your lover Max! *(Beat.)* And your son. What is he now? Fourteen?

IRENE: Yes.

HARRY: An English schoolboy in his English uniform

IRENE: Yes.

HARRY: He'll be in the British army one day. You want him sent to Palestine to shoot his brothers?

IRENE: Don't say that.

HARRY: Why not? And then what will he be? Loyal to the English Crown or loyal to the Jews?

IRENE: He knows who he is.

HARRY: And who is that?

IRENE: You kill me. You know that. *(Silence.)* Look Harry. I want to do more. I want to be in Jaffa. Jerusalem. Haifa.

HARRY: What is this? A Cook's Holiday Tour? Forget it. You're Irene Gold from Golders Green. You've done what's necessary. Thank you and goodnight. *(Silence.)*

IRENE: Is that how you see me Harry? The suburban housewife? I've proved myself haven't I? *(Beat.)* And it's not Golders Green. It's West Hampstead. *(Silence.)*

IRENE: This meeting.

HARRY: What?

IRENE: I need to know what you're planning.

HARRY: No you don't!

IRENE: I came today.

HARRY: Yes, why?

IRENE: I know something…

HARRY: What?

IRENE: …about your 'job'.

HARRY: Oh yes?

IRENE: Whatever it is…

HARRY: What?

IRENE: …you got planned.

HARRY: You know nothing.

IRENE: They know about the Pole.

HARRY: Who knows? What Pole?

IRENE: Oh drop it. I know.

HARRY: You can't.

IRENE: I know he's expected.

HARRY: How could you?

IRENE: Tonight

HARRY: That's rubbish.

IRENE: They've stopped him getting in.

HARRY: Who? Who's stopped who? What are you talking about?

IRENE: The little guy.

HARRY: The little guy! The little guy! The Pole. What is this?

IRENE: They were tipped off. They were waiting for him.

HARRY: Where?

IRENE: France.

HARRY: Where?

IRENE: Marseilles.

HARRY: What do you know?

IRENE: That's all.

HARRY: Who told you? Jesus Christ, now we've got a leak. Jesus. I have to think.

IRENE: You have to call this off.

HARRY: Sol's on his way. Does he know? Hell I need time to think.

IRENE: I need to know what's planned. *(Loudly.)*

HARRY: NO! *(MAX enters.)*

MAX: I made fresh tea.

HARRY: Stinks of cabbage water.

IRENE: Listen to me.

MAX: It's all I could find in your dump.

HARRY: Shut it.

IRENE: Thanks.

MAX: Without milk and sugar? Or without sugar and milk?

IRENE: Russian tea is fine.

HARRY: That's tea without the tea. *(Sound of JOSEPH retching.)*

MAX: Joseph's sick in the bog.

HARRY: And who said Irishmen had charm. Please God the landlady doesn't hear.

MAX: I thought she was deaf.

HARRY: Like a pig in slaughter.

MAX: Feel a bit sick myself. Think I'll go out.

HARRY: You little runt. You can't catch it you know.

MAX: Get some fresh air.

HARRY: Looking like drek you'll be picked up.

MAX: See what's out on the street.

HARRY: Look at you! Find a razor will you.

MAX: Got anything I can sell? *(IRENE passes him her lipstick.)* What do I want with that?

IRENE: Swop it for a shave. *(MAX takes lipstick. Blows her a kiss and makes to leave as JOSEPH comes back in.)*

IRENE: How's the patient?

JOSEPH: Got a guillotine?

IRENE: Lie down.

HARRY: Irene'll look after you.

JOSEPH: *(Yawning.)* Every orifice. Weeping. Shitting. Pissing.

IRENE: Here. *(She takes the black scarf and gives it to JOSEPH.)*

JOSEPH: The chain won't flush. It's all over the place. I disgust myself.

HARRY: Don't we all.

JOSEPH: I don't want the big fella to see me like this.

HARRY: Why isn't he here? It's not like him.

IRENE: Harry we've to talk.

JOSEPH: I'm sweating, you know that. The Ice Age and I'm sweating.

IRENE: You're freezing. Can you light a fire?

HARRY: What do I use for coal?

MAX: Maybe it's a stroke?

JOSEPH: Yesterday. I was examining this forty-year-old woman. She had problems passing stools. Her arse. Like a bunch of grapes.

MAX: Why is he yellow?

IRENE: He's liverish.

HARRY: Lily-livered.

IRENE: Maybe he can't stomach killing. *(A look between IRENE and HARRY.)*

JOSEPH: You calling me a coward?

MAX: You want out of this old man?

IRENE: Sleep now.

JOSEPH: It's January. Why is the sun so sharp?

> *(IRENE sings a Yiddish lullaby.)*
>
> *Shlof mayn kind, mein kroyn, mayn sheyner*
>
> *Schlofze, zunenyu,*
>
> *Shlof, mayn lebn, mayn kaddish eyner*
>
> *Lulinke lu-lu*
>
> *(The door opens. SOLOMON, a tall. elegant man, is standing there in coat, hat and carrying a briefcase.)*

SOL: *(Ironic.)* Musical soirée is it?

HARRY: Joseph is ill.

SOL: No Jew here has time to be ill.

HARRY: This is Max Jacobs.

SOL: Well, well. Since when did we start using dwarfs?

MAX: I'm tall for my family.

SOL: *(Looking at Irene.)* You opening a brothel, Harry?

HARRY: Irene Gold.

SOL: *(Sarcastic.)* Oh I don't believe we have been introduced. Enchanté Madame!

HARRY: She's just passing through.

SOL: Like a dose?

IRENE: I'll go.

SOL: No, do stay. Vodka and gefilte fish all round?

HARRY: She helped us with the gear.

SOL: Good God man, you know the rules. No more than three. We're already four. And now you let her in?

HARRY: She turned up.

JOSEPH: A woman doesn't count.

HARRY: That's right.

IRENE: I'm invisible.

SOL: Not to me.

JOSEPH: I'm going to be sick. *(Irene takes his hand.)*

IRENE: Breathe deeply.

SOL: Ah! The Yiddish Florence Nightingale.

HARRY: Lay off her Professor.

JOSEPH: I need a bucket.

HARRY: Here use this newspaper.

SOL: Why don't we call in the Red Cross?

HARRY: How's the wife?

SOL: We've got work to do. You going to vomit or what?

JOSEPH: One, two three, four,/

HARRY: I'm listening.

JOSEPH: /Five, /

MAX: What about the gear?

JOSEPH: /Six.

SOL: And now Paddy's learning to count.

JOSEPH: I'll be grand.

SOL: Yes but when?

JOSEPH: When I can turn my head and it doesn't explode.

SOL: And when's that?

JOSEPH: Six. Six sixes are thirty-six.

SOL: *(Beat.)* If I'd known I'd've asked Sidney. Maybe I still can.

JOSEPH: Thirty-six wise men. Maybe I'll be fine in a couple of hours. If only I can sleep.

HARRY: We've got a job and he wants to schlof!

JOSEPH: Thirty-six to save the world.

SOL: I should never have let this clown in.

HARRY: We've got to get the gear out. Fast.

IRENE: *(To HARRY.)* You sure?

SOL: This nebbish and now the woman. I don't like it.

IRENE: I'll leave but before I do.

HARRY: Irene!

MAX: She goes I go too.

HARRY: The Jewish Sir Lancelot!

IRENE: I'd better move…

MAX: No!

IRENE: …out on the landing. Wash up the cups.

SOL: Why don't you *(IRENE leaves.)* What the hell do you think you're doing?

HARRY: She's alright.

MAX: What's the story?

SOL: You. Show me your hands.

MAX: What?

SOL: Those nails. Filthy.

MAX: I'll clean them.

SOL: Do you know how crucial this is? Have you any idea? And you come looking like shit.

MAX: I'm sorry boss.

HARRY: Come on Sol. We're ready. So shoot.

SOL: What a bloody mess Harry. Don't you ever clean up?

HARRY: Come on Sol.

SOL: First get the woman out of this place.

JOSEPH: Why am I shivering?

SOL: And you. That's enough. Up on your feet!

HARRY: You were hot a minute ago.

SOL: You. Boychick. How old are you?

MAX: Twenty two.

SOL: You're very thin.

HARRY: He's got no strength.

MAX: Looks are deceptive.

HARRY: Out with it Sol.

MAX: I'm ready.

SOL: Ever bring a man down?

HARRY: The kid worked in the NAAFI.

JOSEPH: *(Singing.) I've got sixpence.*

SOL: You never saw action?

MAX: *(Puts his right hand on his heart.)*. Skips a beat.

SOL: Great. A soldier with a rotten heart.

MAX: Doctors say I've a dodgy ticker. But they're wrong. *(Thumps chest.)* Strong as an ox, not a dicky.

JOSEPH: *(Sings.) To last me all my life.*

HARRY: Will you stop?

MAX: I've crack eyesight. Good enough to fly a Spitfire.

JOSEPH: *I've got tuppence to…*

MAX: I'm an ace shot.

SOL: What about you? Harry. How many you down?

HARRY: Thirty.

SOL: Ak, Ak?

JOSEPH: You were on those big guns?

HARRY: Yes.

SOL: Pointing floodlights into a Messerschmidt isn't the same as face to face.

JOSEPH: *…spend and tuppence to lend*

HARRY: It's ten times worse.

SOL: Question is, are you up to it?

MAX: Harry's an old man!

HARRY: You little shit, I'll kill you.

SOL: *(To MAX.)* Did I ask you?

JOSEPH: *And tuppence to last me…*

HARRY: Who we going for Sol? The Top Man?

MAX: The Top Man!

JOSEPH: Top Man my arse!

SOL: Which of you is the top man for the job?

JOSEPH: I shot a pig once. Outside the Combined General Hospital in Deolali.

MAX: Is it who I think it is?

SOL: A younger man has the best reflexes.

HARRY: That depends.

JOSEPH: After twenty, the brain cells start dying.

MAX: That's right.

HARRY: Your brain's in your arse. *(IRENE enters.)*

IRENE: What's going on here?

MAX: Nothing.

JOSEPH: Keep out of this Irene.

IRENE: *(To HARRY.)* Did you tell them?

SOL: What?

IRENE: What are you planning?

SOL: Time you left, lady

IRENE: Left? Left? First you want to use my house. Then when the stuff's out of it you want rid of me. Why? Because I don't have a tassel dangling between my legs? *(Beat.)* Tell me what's going on.

SOL: Shut up missis!

IRENE: Harry?

HARRY: I don't know.

JOSEPH: Now do I believe that!

MAX: None of us knows.

IRENE: That's a lie.

SOL: Shut it.

JOSEPH: Very gallant I don't think.

IRENE: You taking someone down? Is that why the Pole's/

HARRY: /That's enough!

IRENE: And you think they don't expect this?

JOSEPH: *(Looking at HARRY and SOL.)* You and him. That's it. And what the bloody hell do we do? Just pass the parcel?

MAX: Who's the gun?

IRENE: Who's the target? *(SOL looks at MAX.)*

MAX: It's me! Oh thank you God! My heart! They said it was drek but it's not. It's good! And Sol, he's seen that! He knows I'm the man for the job!

HARRY: You! When I was in the Ak Ak in l941 and they were bombing the hell out the East End, my job was to shine the searchlight up at Jerry. You know what he did? He came down right through the beam. Close to me as you are now. And you know what? I'm still here. You see that. I'm still here.

FAST BLACKOUT.

ACT TWO

FAST LIGHTS UP.

(A minute later.)

HARRY: Well?

JOSEPH: Migraine's gone.

MAX: That was quick.

JOSEPH: I can turn my head without pain. I'm a new man.

MAX: Funny how he's suddenly better.

HARRY: Leave the poor bastard alone.

JOSEPH: What?

MAX: Fancy your chances do you?

JOSEPH: And why not?

MAX: Don't make me piss myself.

SOL: Stop squabbling.

JOSEPH: Me? Did I say anything? Did I?

MAX: The Professor has made his decision.

HARRY: And it's you?

MAX: Well it's not Joseph and it's not you.

HARRY: Really. And how did you work that out?

JOSEPH: You think you're so smart.

SOL: I said stop it! You're all in this together. The individual doesn't matter. Have you learned nothing?

MAX: Yes but there's only one man gets to pull the trigger.

HARRY: And this insignificant schmuck thinks it's him!

SOL: We start fighting and we've all got a date with the hangman. Even you little lady. *(Silence.)* Here's the plan. One drives, one covers and one does the mission.

MAX: But who does the real job?

JOSEPH: First sign of trouble and you'll be running like billy-o.

MAX: I'm not the one who's sick at the thought of action. And two minutes later Moses here is leading the Jews to the Promised Land.

SOL: Stop this. Now!

JOSEPH: And what did you do in the war? Make tea?

MAX: Is it my fault I didn't see active service. Is it?

JOSEPH: Drink a lot of black coffee before the medical did you? "Dicky ticker"?

MAX: You piece of shit

HARRY: Joseph's right. The kid's too much of a risk

IRENE: What do you do Sol?

SOL: What?

IRENE: Thirty-nine to forty-five?

SOL: Me?

IRENE: Did you see action?

SOL: My war record's none of your concern.

IRENE: And why's that?

SOL: Because I signed a paper. What are you doing here Missus? You should be home washing up or making dinner. Does your husband know you're here?

IRENE: You're avoiding my question.

SOL: You want to know about me. Well I am the ears and the eyes. And you are the hands so let's move it.

JOSEPH: There's something I'd like to know.

SOL: And what's that?

JOSEPH: Where exactly do your orders come from?

SOL: If you don't like my command you can leave right now.

JOSEPH: Could be you're just the message boy.

SOL: Yes that's it. I take the messages from the men with tattoos on their arms. Men who hid in graves. *(Takes the coal from the grate.)* This is what it's all about.

JOSEPH: What?

SOL: That's the talk in Whitehall.

MAX: What's coal got to do with anything?

SOL: The country needs fuel. They're even planning to grow nuts in Africa to get it. Britain's on its knees. Coal is power. And what do you think will happen when it runs out?

MAX: What?

SOL: We might as well go back to swinging in the trees. We need new energy.

HARRY: Oil.

JOSEPH: Oh.

SOL: He, who owns the oil, owns the world. Saudi Arabia. Iran. Iraq.

HARRY: So to hell with the little Jew.

SOL: That's why we have to take Palestine by force. Little England has to appease the Arabs. They're the boys with the oil. You think the British Empire will ever let go and give it to the Jews? It has to be taken. India knows it. Ireland knows it. Now it's our turn.

JOSEPH: And the Jews didn't have enough oil to fight the Greeks so they hid inside the Temple where there was only enough oil for one night. But, mysteriously, the oil burned for eight whole days and eight whole nights. Enough time for the Maccabees to defeat Alexander's great empire and take back the Temple in Jerusalem. That was God's miracle. Oil. He helped us then, he'll do it again.

HARRY: God! You and your god. Let me tell you about this great and holy presence.

IRENE: Harry!

HARRY: In Treblinka, when the doors were opened there were thousand of bodies formed into a great pyramid. And guess who was there on these newly-killed Yids?

IRENE: Enough!

HARRY: It was God. It was Javeh. It was El Ohanu. And as he was dancing around, throwing those floppy Yids with their brains and their blood and the guts all over the place, what was he doing our God who chose us above all others? He was laughing so hard that the whole world shook. *(Silence.)*

JOSEPH: We're Jews. We have to believe in something.

HARRY: The gun. The land. Isn't that right Sol?

SOL: The time for God is finished. Harry's right.

JOSEPH: Without God we are nothing.

HARRY: Without Jews God is nothing.

SOL: Our god has to be action.

MAX: I wish I had your brains Sol.

JOSEPH: It's not brains it's public school and Cambridge for you. His family could afford to make him a communist.

SOL: *(Looks at his watch.)* We move in forty minutes. Any man here lacks the balls for direct action, *(To IRENE.)* including you. Leave right now. *(Pause.)*

HARRY: What's the story boss?

JOSEPH: As if you didn't know.

HARRY: Know what?

JOSEPH: Secret meetings. You and him.

HARRY: You've got a fertile imagination.

SOL: Our man.

MAX: Yeh.

HARRY: Yes!

SOL: For God's sake. He's got a private late Cabinet meeting.

MAX: How do you know that?

SOL: Cambridge has its uses.

JOSEPH: What time?

SOL: Midnight.

HARRY: Where?

SOL: Downing Street.

MAX: We taking out the PM then?

IRENE: The Prime Minister?

JOSEPH: You're pulling our legs.

HARRY: You think this is a joke?

SOL: Are you with us 'boyo'?

JOSEPH: I'm listening.

SOL: That's not what I asked.

JOSEPH: I'm with you.

SOL: All the way.

JOSEPH: Jaysus. I'm with you.

SOL: Harry?

HARRY: What?

SOL: How old are you?

HARRY: I don't remember.

SOL: Forty five?

HARRY: Younger.

MAX: I'm twenty two.

HARRY: With the brain of seven.

SOL: We don't need Albert Einstein. Just a mensch with enough balls to pull a trigger. Put this on. *(He opens his briefcase and takes out a British army uniform.)*

MAX: Thanks.

SOL: It'll make you look more manly. *(MAX puts on uniform. When HARRY sees this he puts his on during the dialogue. It should look like a competition to see who can get it on first.)*

HARRY: I'm waiting.

JOSEPH: You tell us bugger all but you've known for what? Weeks?

SOL: Harry covers.

HARRY: That's all?

SOL: Most efficient use of manpower.

JOSEPH: We should have known about this project earlier. Preparation. That's what we need. We can't just take out the top boyo as if we're shooting rabbits.

HARRY: You don't like the way things are done here's your chance to leave.

JOSEPH: I'm going to ignore that. What do you want me to do Sol?

SOL: You drive the motor.

JOSEPH: Oh. *(Everyone looks at JOSEPH.)*

SOL: Don't tell me.

HARRY: You don't drive?

JOSEPH: Not since India.

HARRY: Why's that?

JOSEPH: Over there. I ran into a couple of trees. Lost my confidence. Must've been the climate. I'll be alright here.

HARRY: What a schlemiel.

JOSEPH: Out there, we had chauffeurs. I was a Captain you know.

IRENE: I can drive.

JOSEPH: You!

IRENE: What do you think I did during the war?

JOSEPH: Cromwell tank was it? What do you know. It wasn't Monty but Irene Gold that took out Rommel. Singlehanded.

IRENE: Go to hell.

HARRY: Let me get this straight. You hundred per cent you want Max to do the hit?

SOL: Right.

HARRY: And with Joseph's dexterity behind the wheel, you want me to drive and do the cover?

IRENE: You're not listening to me.

SOL: Joseph can cover too.

JOSEPH: Thanks very much. And who exactly are we taking out? The Prime Minister or his pet poodle?

SOL: And then there's the woman.

IRENE: 'The woman'?

SOL: You'll walk past.

MAX: What for?

SOL: Piece of skirt… One second's distraction and he goes straight to Kingdom Come.

JOSEPH: I love it! Irene Gold the Jewish Mata Hari!

SOL: If you insist on being here you can at least be useful.

IRENE: *(Dryly.)* Thank you.

HARRY: How long do we have?

SOL: Don't want to get there too early. Set of spare pricks. Journey from Brick Lane Harry?

HARRY: Straight down the Commercial Road. Aldgate. Leadenhall Street. Cornhill. Bank. Poultry. Cheapside. St Paul's. Newgate. Farringdon Road. Over Blackfriars Bridge. Down the Lambeth Road. Right for Kennington Lane straight to Vauxhall. Wandsworth Road.

JOSEPH: Wandsworth Road! Why not Number Ten?

SOL: How long?

JOSEPH: I'm sure I asked a question. Why does everyone ignore me?

HARRY: This time of night? Thirty minutes max. Though with the fog maybe we should give it an hour.

SOL: We move in a few minutes.

JOSEPH: Jaysus!

SOL: Now the logistics. You're parked on the other side of the street. Nobody notices a black cab. You'll need a quarter of an hour at the most to check the area. Any longer could be suspicious. It's ten past nine now, we need to move it. He'll be at dinner in Wandsworth til the car comes to pick him up at eleven. Latest eleven fifteen

HARRY: And where are we?

SOL: There's a lot of garden, Max waits in the bushes. You're watching in the cab. His driver pulls up outside his house. He goes to knock on the door. Our man comes out. They both walk down the path to the official motor. Chauffeur opens the door for him. At that moment the skirt walks past. Have you got some perfume?

IRENE: *(Sarcastic.)* Chanel or Dior?

SOL: He looks at the skirt and, in that second, when his reflex is in his dick, Max takes him out.

HARRY: The driver, is he armed?

SOL: No.

JOSEPH: Will someone tell me who we're doing?

SOL: You'll find out.

JOSEPH: I get it. We scare the PM's chauffeur. Put them on high alert.

HARRY: What about a heavy? It's not just our man and the driver is it?

SOL: There'll be one bodyguard.

HARRY: And is he walking with the driver?

MAX: What if there's two men?

SOL: We've checked. It's one

HARRY: Is the heavy standing in the road by the car or walking down the path to the front door with the driver?

SOL: Could be either.

JOSEPH: You don't know?

SOL: They change the routine.

MAX: But what if he's got more than one heavy with him?

SOL: If they've got two, so have we. It's even.

HARRY: No. If the driver's armed and there are two bodyguards we're outnumbered. How do we even know Joseph can shoot straight?

JOSEPH: Migraine's gone. My vision's twenty twenty.

SOL: Stop worrying. The driver won't be carrying anything. And we, we've got our beauty queen as a surprise.

HARRY: Yes but Irene's only going to take his attention for a second.

SOL: That's what counts. In this fog they won't see clear. He'll smell woman. He won't smell you.

HARRY: But will he smell her in the fog?

SOL: I didn't think of that. You sure you've no perfume?

HARRY: What's the risk level?

IRENE: High.

SOL: Low.

HARRY: How's that?

SOL: They expect action in Jerusalem not on home ground.

IRENE: They're already on their guard.

JOSEPH: What about moles?

HARRY: You trying to tell us something?

JOSEPH: You bastard.

SOL: Let's not waste time.

HARRY: Go through it again. From when he leaves the house and the getting into the car, we've got what? Two? Three minutes?

SOL: Right.

HARRY: And in that two, three minutes Bevin's down.

MAX: Bevin?

JOSEPH: Ernest Bevin. *(Beat.)* The Foreign Secretary!

MAX: Fuck me!

HARRY: The Right Honourable Ernest Bevin. Couldn't happen to worthier scum.

IRENE: This is crazy. They'll expect him to be at risk

MAX: Bevin! The dog in his kennel! I love it.

JOSEPH: So you did know you bastard. You've known for days isn't that right?

HARRY: What's it to you? Soldiers obey orders.

IRENE: Even when it's suicide?

JOSEPH: You think you're above the rest of us do you? Two of you ganging up. I've been involved as long as you. Give Paddy the donkey work but not real action.

HARRY: And who brought you in to the movement?

JOSEPH: You did.

HARRY: Which means?

JOSEPH: I don't know.

HARRY: It means you're junior to me, you understand?

JOSEPH: Junior? We're creating a new army, that's what you said. No officers, no hierarchy no, fucking English class

SOL: Here. *(Has a small bottle of Scotch in pocket. Offers it round.)*

HARRY: Where you get that?

SOL: L'chaim! Now I suggest you all calm down. Save your spunk for the job.

JOSEPH: The Foreign Secretary!

MAX: It's brilliant. Bleedin' brilliant!

JOSEPH: That bastard puts us in camps in Cyprus and we take him out on home turf. That's what I call chutzpah!

IRENE: They'll burn out every Jew in England. *(They all look at her.)*

HARRY: What?

IRENE: Is that what you want?

HARRY: What do you suggest? Do nothing?

IRENE: Did I say that?

HARRY: Expulsion. Inquisition. Auto da Fé. Pogrom. Deportation. Internment. Is that what you want!

IRENE: You take out the Foreign Secretary, they'll round us up in the streets.

HARRY: You can take the girl out of the ghetto but you can't take the ghetto out of the girl.

IRENE: It's one thing running guns through France to Palestine but taking out their top gun in a South London suburb.

MAX: It's wonderful!

IRENE: Bevin's not Goebbels. The English are not the Nazis.

HARRY: Aren't they?

IRENE: Just listen to yourself.

HARRY: At least the Nazis wanted to give the Jews a land.

IRENE: I'm trying to save your life.

HARRY: Don't!

JOSEPH: Uganda…

MAX: And now the English/

JOSEPH: Maybe we should've gone there.

MAX: /want to give our country to the stinking Arabs and to hell with the stinking Jews.

JOSEPH: In Palestine the public schoolboys are fucking the Arab boys. We don't let them do that to us. Why should they like us?

IRENE: They're on top alert. We know that.

SOL: No wonder with you breaking the rules.

IRENE: The mission must be called off.

SOL: Who gives the orders here? A piece of skirt?

IRENE: I pity you. I pity all of us.

MAX: I pity the spotty soldier out in Palestine/

JOSEPH: Maybe she's right/

MAX: /he's got no stinking choice but Ernie Bevin, he's the man behind the policy.

JOSEPH: Maybe it's doomed. Are we Jews or terrorists?

HARRY: Why are you here Joseph?

JOSEPH: I save lives, you know that.

HARRY: Ah the Hippocratic oath!

JOSEPH: What's wrong with that?

HARRY: What happens when a baby with an enlarged head is born? What do you do when from the womb comes a monster?

JOSEPH: What's that got to do with this?

HARRY: I'd like to know.

JOSEPH: This is not the time.

HARRY: Oh I think it is *(Pause.)*

JOSEPH: When we deliver an infant that's crippled… I can't say…

HARRY: Yes you can.

JOSEPH: It gets left, naked on the sink with the window open.

HARRY: And what do you tell the mother?

JOSEPH: Sorry missis. The child was born dead.

HARRY: And what is the difference between what you do and this?

JOSEPH: Bevin's not a new born child. He has a wife and children.

HARRY: I'm crying here!

139

SOL: Which is your country, Joseph?

JOSEPH: Palestine.

HARRY: Or England? You with your precious British passport!

JOSEPH: We'll end up shot by like the boyos in the Dublin
Post Office in l916. All those brave Irish lads. Dead. And
they still don't have their country.

MAX: But we're still talking about them. They're heroes!

JOSEPH: You want us to become martyrs like Patrick Pearse.
What the bloody hell use is that?

HARRY: And you want to die an old man in your own bed!

SOL: I am not sure we can trust you Joseph.

JOSEPH: I'm here aren't I? I've done as much for the cause as
Harry.

SOL: A Yid with a conscience is no use here.

JOSEPH: I'm a doctor. Bevin's planning a new health system to
save millions of poor people's lives.

SOL: That's Nye Bevan. What's wrong with you?

HARRY: In nineteen forty, forty one, while we were here, in
internment camps or being bombed, what were you doing?
Drinking char with Mahatma Gandhi?

JOSEPH: I'm not saying turn the other cheek.

HARRY: Aren't you?

SOL: Come on!

JOSEPH: I want to do it. I want to rip that bastard apart but
inside I'm shaking.

MAX: What's this clown doing here?

HARRY: You should never have joined us.

JOSEPH: How could I know? *(HARRY puts on his British Army
hat.)*

HARRY: I'll do the job. The kid's my apprentice.

MAX: Apprentice? You stinking bastard.

IRENE: Stop this *(HARRY goes to fight MAX but SOL stops the struggle.)*

SOL: Are you completely crazy? Are you? *(Silence. HARRY turns his back on the group.)*

IRENE: If we go ahead.

HARRY: If? If? There is no if.

IRENE: If we do, I want it known I'm not against this action. Not at all. In fact I rather admire its daring. But the Pole's been stopped at the airport. I say do it when it's cooled down. A week or two.

SOL: What do you know. You know nothing. We need to prepare. Now!

HARRY: Irene can drive. You said you wanted to be more involved. Well?

IRENE: If you have to go then I'm with you.

HARRY: Even if you think it's suicide?

IRENE: With you, I never played safe *(They look at one another.)*

HARRY: And the job? The kid? Or me?

SOL: Sorry Harry. *(HARRY turns as if to go for MAX but stops himself. Pause.)*

SOL: Time to clear this place up. Where's the gear? *(HARRY goes to get the bag.)*

HARRY: *(Kissing the bag.)* Bon voyage my darling. *(SOL takes it.)*

SOL: I'll be back in five minutes. What time do you all have? Nine thirty? We're out this door at nine forty. *(SOL exits.)*

MAX: I've been chosen and you're jealous.

HARRY: You say that to me? You've taken exactly what you wanted all your life. Nina thinks you shit sunshine. And Johnny should've strapped you long ago.

MAX: You leave my father out of this.

HARRY: Johnny? He's a lobos of the first degree.

MAX: You're not fit to wipe his arse.

HARRY: Shall I tell you about the man you call your father.

MAX: What?

IRENE: Don't!

MAX: Don't what?

JOSEPH: Have you got a uniform for me?

HARRY: You'll stay here, guard the shop.

JOSEPH: And who'll make me?

MAX: What about my father?

HARRY: Nothing.

IRENE: Your father's a good man.

MAX: What's this all about?

IRENE: Your mother loved him.

MAX: And why shouldn't she?

HARRY: He's not all she loved.

MAX: What?

IRENE: Stop this now!

HARRY: You heard me.

MAX: What are you saying?

JOSEPH: I loved a girl once.

MAX: You calling my mother a whore?

JOSEPH: I spent one night with her. How was I to know she was a professional?

HARRY: A whore. To love more than one man, is that a whore?

IRENE: That's enough Harry.

MAX: You started something, get on with it.

JOSEPH: She asks me for a few bob. I just thought she was just short of cash for the gas meter.

IRENE: He'll be back in a minute and you're still not ready.

JOSEPH: And then it clicked.

MAX: You and my mother. Is that what you're saying?

JOSEPH: Thought I could make her love me.

IRENE: *(To MAX.)* You have to finish getting dressed.

JOSEPH: I waited outside and men kept coming in and out. In and out. After that I didn't even want the old hand job.

MAX: I'm not moving til you tell me.

JOSEPH: Makes me feel like a baboon.

HARRY: Now!

HARRY: Nina. Your mother. She didn't used to be fat. She went in and out as a girl should. Back then, even I was thin, just like you.

IRENE: Harry, that's enough.

MAX: What are you saying?

HARRY: Your father.

MAX: What about him?

HARRY: Your're looking at him.

MAX: That's a lie. A stinking shitty lie.

HARRY: And now you want to be a hero. It's all right. I'll let you.

MAX: You'll let me!

HARRY: But first you've got to fight me.

MAX: You? A pathetic old man!

HARRY: Beat me and you can beat anyone!

MAX: You know what you are to me? Nothing.

HARRY: You don't want to fight me then go home to mummy. Get the hell out of here. You may be Nina's son but you've not got your father's balls.

MAX: You're not my father.

HARRY: You've got your mother's eyes.

MAX: What?

HARRY: And her nose.

MAX: Leave my mother out of your filthy mouth.

HARRY: But you're a stubborn piece of shit. Just like me.

MAX: Like you? If I thought you were any part of me I'd go out and kill myself.

HARRY: Go on. Go home nancy boy.

MAX: Nancy boy!

HARRY: You're soft inside. You're not a fighter. You got my blood but not my guts.

MAX: I know your game. You think I'm a klutz but I can see what you're up to

HARRY: Oh yeh?

MAX: Yes! You pretending you're my father to make me think my mother's a whore to make me crazy. Sol comes back and sees me way out of control. He gets shot of me and you get the honour.

HARRY: Honour? It's a job to be done. A historical imperative. But whatever you do, you stay, you go, I'm proud to tell everyone that you're my son. *(HARRY moves around him tauntingly. MAX won't fight.)*

HARRY: Man to man. Come on, come on! You'll win. You're younger and stronger. Come on son.

MAX: My mother wouldn't touch you.

HARRY: We'll do this together.

MAX: She's a decent woman. Isn't she?

HARRY: I'll cover you with my life.

MAX: You and her! I can't bear it. You're lying. Tell me it's a lie.

HARRY: Come on Isaac.

MAX: My mother wouldn't let you near her.

HARRY: Look at that nose. It's mine.

MAX: You'd say anything.

HARRY: Your grandfather's mouth.

MAX: You should be dead Harry. When the Nazis were gassing Yid after Yid after Yid, you know what? I wish they'd gassed you too! *(HARRY lunges at MAX. They have a vicious fight but the wrestling becomes an embrace.)*

HARRY: That's my boy. That's my Maxie. Yes, go for it. *(HARRY suddenly hits him. SOL rushes in.)*

SOL: Turn the light off.

HARRY: What?

SOL: Quick.

JOSEPH: What's going on? *(Blackout.)*

SOL: Got a match?

IRENE: Here *(Lights a match.)*

HARRY: What's up?

SOL: There are two men outside. Watching the house.

JOSEPH: Jaysus.

HARRY: Calling it off then.

SOL: We do nothing.

IRENE: Max isn't moving.

HARRY: What?

IRENE: I can't feel a pulse.

SOL: Keep the noise down.

HARRY: Max, Max. Stop kidding around. Come on kid. Come on son. Max. Say something. Come on. I love you, you bastard. You know that. Hit me. I want to see you go for an upper cut.

IRENE: He's not breathing.

HARRY: Come on Maxie. Give me a jab. Right here. On the shnozzle. Come on!

SOL: I said shut it.

HARRY: Look me in the eyes and then catch me on the chin. *(Takes his hand and tries to make a fist from it.)* Come on Maxie. My son. Do it. Hit me.

BLACKOUT

NINEVEH

Nineveh is dedicated to Sally Mijit.

Nineveh by Julia Pascal premiered 16 April 2013 at Riverside Studios with the following cast:

RICHIE	Gethin Alderman
JOHNNY	Nabil Stuart
JOEL	Yaron Shavit
CHANCE	John Kamau

Directed by Ailin Conant
Designed by Claire Lyth
Produced by Theatre Témoin

Characters

JOHNNY
The leader

RICHIE
The eternal student

JOEL
The clown

CHANCE
The kid

Four former soldiers.

Chance should be African.

(Note the testimony which was the source of this play was gathered in Kashmir, Israel, Lebanon and Rwanda but the text is not specific to these countries. Original research was undertaken by Ailin Conant in 2012.)

The time is today.

The set is claustrophic. It is rough and full of planking. The design resembles the ribs of a ship.

OVERTURE

Sound: As the audience comes in there is the sound of water.

LIGHTS

BLACKOUT

Sound: Storm.

The storm subsides in the blackout. Within the soundscape there are strange noises that later are revealed to be part of traumatic memories.

IN BLACKOUT

OVERTURE/PROLOGUE

RICHIE: Go!

LIGHTS UP (Fast)

RICHE, JOEL and JOHNNY are all jumping at different speeds. It looks like a game. They are dodging bullets. There is a voice mix of Swahili, Urdu, Arabic, Hebrew. The male voices come in one at a time. They are training soldiers. One by one the actors fall down as if dead. They get up and fall repeatedly. The shouting of instructions carries on through the movement. At times the languages mix so the effect is of Babel. As they keep moving

BLACKOUT

LIGHTS UP (Fade)

The actors are in a different position. Apart from the heavy breathing it is as if nothing has happened and they have been in this place for a long time.

JOHNNY: Get on!

JOEL: What?

JOHNNY: Just do it.

JOEL: What?

JOHNNY: Move!

JOEL: It's not my turn.

JOHNNY: I said move!

JOEL: I'm tired.

JOHNNY: He's tired! Poor baby!

JOEL: Stop that.

JOHNNY: Unbelievable.

JOEL: OK. OK.

> *(JOEL gets a bucket. He is about to bale out the water but, instead, he puts it on his head.)*

JOHNNY: Very funny.

> *(JOHNNY kicks him. JOEL falls forward.)*

JOEL: Why do you do that?

JOHNNY: Is baby hurt?

JOEL: I've got/

JOHNNY: /a bullet in my ass. Please Johnny don't hurt me!

JOEL: I have.

JOHNNY: Get working pretty boy. Pretty Joelie.

JOEL: I'm not pretty.

JOHNNY: No. You're not.

> *(Lights flicker to Blackout.)*

<u>*Movement sequence.*</u>

> *The men are clearly in what seems to be the hull of a ship. They hold on to one another in fear. It throws them around. There is the SOUND of wind. There are three different positions held as they struggle to keep secure.*

> *LIGHTS slowly up.*

JOEL: When will she stop?

JOHNNY: When she sees land.

JOEL: And when's that?

JOHNNY: You're like a child. Questions, questions, questions.

> *(Beat while JOEL thinks what to do. He buckets out the water.)*

JOEL: How come you never do it?

JOHNNY: I do plenty.

JOEL: But I never see you.

JOHNNY: When you sleep, I work.

JOEL: *(Looking at RICHIE.)* What about him?

RICHIE: What? What?

JOEL: Well, do you?

RICHIE: I'm busy.

JOEL: *(Mimicking him.)* Busy, I'm busy!

RICHIE: I'm reading. Try it. Or did you go blind playing with your dick?

JOEL: Go to hell. *(Beat.)* What's the book?

RICHIE: As if it matters to you!

JOEL: I can read. You think I can't *(To JOHNNY. Over-emphatically)* Tell him I can.

JOHNNY: Work, boy.

(JOEL grabs the book and moves it around. RICHIE tries to get it back. JOEL is faster than him.)

JOEL: What is it? I know. *(Looking at the cover)* Shakespeare!

JOHNNY: Shakespeare! What do you know of Shakespeare!

JOEL: I know plenty.

RICHIE: Name one play. *(Silence.)*

JOEL: I know!

JOHNNY: Oh yes?

JOEL: *Woman With An Ass!*

RICHIE: Cretin!

JOEL: I'm not a cretin. *(Over-emphatically.)* Tell him I'm not a cretin. She's a fairy. And there's/

JOHNNY: Get on with your work.

JOEL: /a boy. He's Indian. You tell him!

(JOEL looks as if he is about to fight RICHIE.)

JOEL: When I get out of here I'll go to Hollywood and be a star! You'll see!

(RICHIE laughs for a long time.)

JOEL: And you, you'll always be nothing. Nothing. Do you hear me?

RICHIE: To be an actor you got to know how to read!

JOEL: I know what's in your book! It's not Shakespeare. I was kidding.

RICHIE: Oh yeh?

JOEL: The Kama, the Kama *(Beat.)* something.

RICHIE: Yes that's it. *(Mocking.)* The Kama something.

JOEL: You are always putting me down. But I'm as good as you.

RICHIE: How's that?

JOEL: Stuff/

JOHNNY: What stuff?

JOEL: *(Looks around.)* /with a knife

RICHIE: What with a knife?

JOEL: I.....I ....did....

JOHNNY: You?

JOEL: I am not, nobody like you think. My father....

JOHNNY: You had a father?

JOEL: How dare you!

RICHIE: Your mother was too thick to know who was up and at her!

JOEL: She's....she's...not.....thick. My father...

JOHNNY: What about him?

JOEL: he, he, he wants....

JOHNNY: Get on with it! You got something to say so say it.

JOEL: *(Suddenly violent.)* Not a boy! A man!! In a ditch.

JOHNNY: What you going on about?

RICHIE: With a knife? In a ditch?

JOEL: *(As if repeating someone else's instructions.)*

That's what men do.

JOHNNY: What?

JOEL: *(As if repeating someone else's instructions)*

Prove it!

Get in that ditch. *(Beat.)*

And....and....I go down, go down, go down. *(Silence.)*

(Stuttering.) I.....

RICHIE: Did what?

JOEL: What ….......they …......

JOHNNY: What?

(LIGHTS flash. They are thrown to one side.)

JOHNNY: Bitch going to kill us!

RICHIE: Why are ships always female?

JOEL: I fell and it hurts *(Beat.)*

Is this sea water? It doesn't smell like it.

(JOEL buckets.)

RICHIE: What's to eat?

JOHNNY: Fish.

JOEL: Fish. Fish. Fish. *(He buckets.)*

But not with a knife. *(Beat.)*

Not at first.

JOHNNY: I hate fish. *(Beat.)* If we were Japanese we wouldn't mind.

JOEL: *(Stops.)* I got it!

JOHNNY: Keep working.

JOEL: Sutra! Kama Sutra!

RICHIE: Kama Sutra! Where did you learn that? You never even been with a woman!

JOEL: Who said that? You say that? I've got a wife.

RICHIE: Is she fat?

JOEL: Fat? Fat?

RICHIE: She's fat!

JOHNNY: Legs like an elephant's!

RICHIE: Fat belly down to her knees!

JOHNNY: Fat tits like a cow!

RICHIE: Fat neck, fat nose. Even her ears are fat!

JOEL: I hate you!

RICHIE: Oh no?

JOEL: She's not fat. She's *(Beat.)* round.

JOHNNY: Round?

JOEL: Fleshy.

RICHIE: Obese!

JOEL: Voluptuous!

RICHIE: Fat! Fat! Fat! *(Beat.)* The knife in the ditch?

JOHNNY: Yes?

(JOEL runs from one side of the stage to the other as if training.)

RICHIE: Come on.

JOEL: *Row, row, row your boat.*

JOHNNY: Stop it.

JOEL: *Life is but, life is but, life is.*

RICHIE: *(Screaming.)* Tell us!

JOEL: What?

JOHNNY: What you did. What you did. What you did. Not with a knife.

JOEL: No. Not with a knife.

JOHNNY: How then?

JOEL: How what?

JOHNNY: First time. Killing.

JOEL: Go away

JOHNNY: You have to tell me. Do it! Do it!! Do it!!!

(JOHNNY and RICHIE push him continually and his speech comes through the action of trying to resist them.)

JOEL: Got to be strong. Got to be fit. You never know what's coming. Got to be ready.

(The voice of his father in his head.)

Do it boy. Show us you are a man! *(Singing) Life is but, life is but, life is* Get in the ditch! Smash your fist in his nose. *Row, row* I want to see the blood gushing from his eyes *your boat merrily* Show me the man! Do it! Do it!! Do it!!! Take the knife! ....*down the stream down, down, down*

(JOEL looks up and pauses. He starts bucketing in a frenzy.)

Take the knife. Hard, hard to cut through the skin and the stuff *Life is but* and the guts and the blood all over me-must-have-cut-the- *down the stream* jugular-hot-on-my-face-they-didn't-tell-me- *but a dream* and-I'm-screaming-and-his-blood-in-my-mouth.

(JOEL stops bucketing. Puts the bucket on his head and dances wildly.)

Row, row, down, down merrily, merrily life is but life is life is but merrily down, down

(JOEL starts bucketing fast and singing. The effect is that of a stuck record.)

(JOHNNY smells the bucket.)

JOHNNY: It's not sea water. It's acid.

RICHIE: My head is killing me. *(A steel rod is thrown onstage.)*

JOHNNY: What the hell?

RICHIE: Who threw that in?

JOEL: Jotsam.

RICHIE: Jotsam?

JOEL: And fletsam. What do you know? You know nothing!

JOHNNY: Cretin!

RICHIE: What else is coming*? (Shouting at the outside world.)* Champagne?

JOHNNY: Kebab? We want meat! Beef. Chicken. Horse. Camel. Lion. Unicorn.

RICHIE: Unicorn?

(JOEL picks up the tube. He looks down it. He plays with it as if he is a circus performer. During the next text between RICHIE and JOHNNY, he is clowning.)

(Sound of water over thirty seconds. Nobody speaks).

RICHIE: How did you get here?

JOHNNY: I don't remember.

RICHIE: Try.

JOHNNY: Nothing.

RICHIE: Try harder.

JOHNNY: Sometimes when I sleep I hear/

RICHIE: /voices. Me too.

JOHNNY: A man's.

RICHIE: Who?

JOHNNY: That's it. Who?

RICHIE: Words? You get words?

JOHNNY: Sounds.

RICHIE: Me too.

JOHNNY: It's just for a few seconds/

RICHIE: /in the day

JOHNNY: Yes!

RICHIE: and then?

JOHNNY: Nothing.

RICHIE: Did the man up there *(Pointing to the sky.)*

JOHNNY: put us here?

JOEL: What man? *(Beat.)* Oh him!

RICHIE: I don't believe in all that.

JOHNNY: Me neither.

JOEL: That's why. He's punishing you.

JOHNNY: This god they talk about. He's always punishing us.

JOEL: We fell in.

JOHNNY: We didn't fall. How could we all fall?

JOEL: Fell in to get saved?

JOHNNY: From what?

RICHIE: From what?

JOHNNY: From knowing too much.

RICHIE: How can you know too much? You can't know enough. I'll never live long enough to know all there is to know. To feel all there is to feel. You know that. It kills me that. Frigging kills me.

JOHNNY: You think it's all in books? What about life?

RICHIE: Life stinks. But you. You, I know. *(Beat.)*

You came here after The Great Storm.

JOHNNY: Did I?

RICHIE: I was here. Alone. With The Book. Then there was the Great Storm followed by The Great Waves. Then there was you.

JOHNNY: The Great Waves. I never heard them. What about you? How did you get here?

RICHIE: I just woke up here. And then you two. Let me read, will you?

JOEL: *(JOEL looks at the metal pipe.)*

(Reading.) Made in Nineveh! Where is that?

(JOHNNY takes the pipe and examines it.)

JOHNNY: I thought you can't read!

JOEL: You thought! You thought!

JOHNNY: Made in Nineveh. How did you get that? Says *Heven-in-Eden*.

JOEL: *Edam*. Dutch. Like the cheese. Maybe we are in a dyke? Or a fjord? We can see the midnight sun.

RICHIE: That's Norway dummy!

JOHNNY: You think we in some pleasure cruiser? This is a junk. And someone's locked us in the hold. Cretin!

JOEL: I am not/

RICHIE: /a cretin!

JOEL: Leave me alone. I know where we are. *And you know nothing.*

RICHIE: Question is who would lock us up. Who would do that?

JOHNNY: *(Looking down the tube.)* Nineveh. Heven. In.

JOEL: Where is that? Japan? Kashmir!

RICHIE: No.

JOEL: Rwanda? Istut-Utuh. Ynamreg. Muigleb.

JOHNNY: Muigleb. Belgium!

JOEL: Measure the heads. Isn't that what they did in Africa?

RICHIE: Nineveh. Where is that?

JOEL: Let me think. Ruled by the Phoenicians. The Ottomans. Syria to the North.

RICHIE: Lebanon!

JOEL: Nonabel! I was going to say that. Why do you have to spoil it?

RICHIE: Because you're slow

JOHNNY: Eden's not in Lebanon. It's in Israel.

RICHIE: So is Gehenna. That's Hell.

JOEL: You're wrong. Both of you.

RICHIE: Are we?

JOEL: Made in Nineveh – that's *(He stutters.)*

RICHIE: Assyria.

JOEL: I hate you!

JOHNNY: *(Beat.)* Iraq!

JOEL: *(Deflated.)* Qari? How do you know that?

JOHNNY: I read. *(Silence.)*

    (Sniffing.) Definitely acid.

RICHIE: How long have we been here?

JOHNNY: Twenty years?

JOEL: Three days.

RICHIE: Three days? How do you know?

JOEL: *(Looks at his watch).* Says so.

JOHNNY: Let me see. Hands are stuck. Battery's dead.

JOEL: Dead? But we can't die. God wouldn't let us!

    (RICHIE laughs a long time. Sound of water. Silence. Slow working from the men.)

JOEL: Jesus was in the wilderness three days.

JOHNNY: Oh he thinks he's Jesus does he?

RICHIE: Jesus is Jupiter. King of the gods.

JOHNNY: Yeh.

JOEL: The Egyptians invented God. Ak-ak-ak-ak-ak natan. He died and came back- Aknahtan! Sun-God. *(Pause.)* You think we'll see the sun again?

    (Sound of water.)

JOEL: We'll never get out of here. The men who locked us up here. They'll never come back.

RICHIE: Shut up.

JOEL: We're stuck. We'll die here.

RICHIE: We have food.

JOEL: Fish. Fish. Fish. *(Beat.)* My aunt ate her sister.

RICHIE: What?

JOEL: In the Last Great War.

RICHIE: Did she taste good?

JOEL: Maybe I will eat you. *(Beat.)* We'll never get out. Will we.

JOHNNY: Shut up.

JOEL: You so clever, you get us out. Or you? With your clever book. What's in it?

JOHNNY: Don't tell me I'm going to die here with this cretin.

RICHE: We have oxygen.

JOEL: And when it runs out? *(Pause.)* Your book. *(To JOHNNY.)* Tell him to give me the book! *(JOHNNY attacks JOEL. He beats him to the ground. RICHIE pulls him off.)*

RICHIE: That's enough. *(JOHNNY looks as if he will hit RICHIE. He decides not to.)*

Movement scene:

They are thrown on the ground suddenly. The following dialogue happens as they are still fighting to remain stable.

JOEL: Oh God oh God oh God!

RICHIE: It's not a ship.

JOHNNY: What?

RICHIE: We're at the bottom of the sea.

JOHNNY: What?

RICHIE: It's a sub.

JOEL: Unterseefisch.

RICHIE: Unterseefisch. That's German.

JOEL: Is it?

JOHNNY: How you know that word?

JOEL: I don't.

RICHIE: It came out of your mouth.

JOEL: Yes. But I don't know it.

RICHIE: That doesn't make sense.

JOHNNY: A submarine doing what?

RICHIE: Spying? Hiding?

JOHNNY: From what?

JOEL: Who sends me these strange words?

JOHNNY: What?

JOEL: Voices in my head. Different languages. Backwards. Sideways.

RICHIE: All your life?

JOEL: It starts when I am with animals. I know what they are saying. I don't know how. And I can tell we are in an Unterseefisch, whatever that is.

(A box is thrown in. CD player. Sudden violin music. Paganani '24 Caprices'. Op 1.Number 9.)

What's that? You hear that? *(JOEL dances wildly. The others look.)*

JOEL: Why are we here?

JOHNNY: Why? Why? Why? Do I know?

JOEL: You two smart punks, you think of something then.

RICHIE: You're right. We'll never get out. We'll die here. In this place. We'll rot.

Sound: Paganini mixes with storm and is drowned by it. Storm whips up and winds howl. RICHIE, JOEL, JOHNNY are thrown and end up holding on to one another. Sound mix with drumming. Lights flicker to Blackout. Lights flicker on. JOEL, JOHNNY, RICHIE are exhausted.

RICHIE: The engine's dead. Bottom of the sea. End of the world.

JOEL: I can hear drumming.

RICHIE: Nobody will ever find us now.

JOEL: Listen.

RICHIE: Nothing.

JOEL: It's Japanese.

RICHIE: What is it with you and Japan?

JOEL: Kamikaze. *(JOEL makes the sound of a plane being hit and dropping from the sky.)*

JOHNNY: What's that?

RICHIE: What?

JOHNNY: Under that pile. *(RICHIE lifts it. There is a terrified boy.)* How did you get here?

JOEL: Who are you? Are there more? Armies of kids come to take our food. Breathe our air. Soldiers. Come to kill us.

JOHNNY: Who are you? *(CHANCE shields himself in anticipation of being beaten.)*

JOEL: What's wrong?

RICHIE: Talk boy!

JOHNNY: It's OK. We won't hurt you.

JOEL: Why doesn't he say something?

JOHNNY: *(Yelling.)* Talk!

RICHIE: Maybe there's a reason for him being here?

JOHNNY: Reason? What reason? *(Sound of water.)*

JOEL: I know who he is.

RICHIE: Who?

JOEL: He's the son of Noah!

JOHNNY: We're not in a frigging ark.

JOEL: Then if we're not in an ark, where are we? I know. Hell?

RICHIE: Hell doesn't exist.

JOEL: Yes it does. I saw a picture once. These angels with their feet in the air and wild dogs with bloody teeth waiting to eat them. I hate bloody dogs. D-o-g. G-o-d. It's the same word backwards!!

RICHIE: Were there fires in the picture?

JOEL: Big flames and the heads were pointing down. The men and women, they were about to be burned alive.

RICHIE: *(As if to a child.)* So it was hot?

JOEL: Yes.

RICHIE: And here. Is it hot?

JOEL: It's cold.

RICHIE: So is it hell? *(Silence.)*

JOEL: When I get out, I'm going to the mountains. Learn to ski. Get all the girls.

JOHNNY: Oh the mountains now? Hollywood will be bereft! *(They all move up and down.)*

RICHIE: What was that?

JOHNNY: The sub's hit the bottom.

RICHIE: It's not a sub. No periscope.

JOHNNY: There wouldn't be one in the hold. You supposed to be smart!

RICHIE: If it's not a boat and it's not a sub, what is it?

JOEL: Let's get out. Make a hole. Swim. Crawl. Butterfly. Breast.

JOHNNY: She got fat ones? Your wife?

JOEL: Stop talking about her.

JOHNNY: Then work cretin.

JOEL: My father threw me in once. *(He makes strange movements.)* I can paddle til someone comes.

RICHIE: And who would that be?

JOEL: There are people out there. Sailors. Tell me there are men there!

RICHIE: Are there?

JOEL: The boy. He knows. He came with sailors. Didn't you? *(Turns on the boy)* Get up!

CHANCE hides. JOEL, JOHNNY and RICHIE round on him and make him stand. Gradually they force his face into the light. His lips are sewn.

JOHNNY: Well, well.

RICHIE: That's something!

JOEL: Would you look at that!

JOEL: Who did it to you? *(Silence.)*

RICHIE: He can't tell you, cretin.

JOEL: Oh.

JOHNNY: What the hell is this?

RICHIE: You got scissors somewhere?

JOHNNY: Sure. And antiseptic. And cotton wool!

JOEL: What do we do? *(Pause.)* You think there is just us alive in the world. And him.

RICHIE: Could be. *(Beat.)*

JOHNNY: Come on. The water. It's rising.

Movement scene:

(The three bucket. There is a symmetry to their motion. CHANCE watches. Light change. Sound of drumming in the distance. JOHNNY, JOEL and RICHIE listen. Spotlight on CHANCE. He mimes a story.)

RICHIE: What is this?

JOEL: Do it again. *(CHANCE does. JOEL 'translates'.)*

JOEL: A baby is abandoned in the jungle by his family. A stranger finds him and the boy is taken to the army.

When he is nine, he is forced to be a soldier or else he will get no food. He learns to use a Kalishnakov.

The enemy captures him and they cut off both his arms. He goes back to his family who see that he cannot work and they throw him in the river.

He is swallowed by an enormous fish, who carries him all the way to A-m-e-r-i-c-a.

When he is there he grows back his arms. He becomes a pilot.

He flies to the jungle to see his family. Now he is perfect and rich, they want him back.

He opens his arms to them and, when he can feel their breath on his cheek, with his new arms, with his new hands, he slaps their face.

RICHIE: And?

JOEL: And? *(CHANCE stops and sits. Sound: The low level drumming stops.)*

JOEL: What's your name? *(CHANCE hides.)*

JOHNNY: Take off his shirt. *(RICHIE does. CHANCE tries to stop him and fails.)*

JOEL: There is a label.

RICHIE: What does it say?

JOHNNY: *(JOHNNY reads.)* Someone's having us on.

RICHIE: Show me. *(JOEL takes it.)*

JOEL: *Made in Nineveh.* Him too.

RICHIE: What's your name kid? *(CHANCE turns away. JOHNNY pushes him.)*

JOHNNY: Oh shit he can't talk.

JOEL: Tell me. *(CHANCE writes backwards in the air. E C N A H C.)*

JOHNNY: ECNAHC. What's that?

JOEL: ECNAHC-CHANCE.

RICHIE: How come he writes backwards too? You know him? *(CHANCE grabs a steel rod and starts 'shooting' the others. He makes the noise of a gun. JOHNNY and RICHIE jump on him.)*

JOHNNY: Who sewed your lips?

RICHIE: Tell us or we won't let you go. *(CHANCE tries to fight them and then gives up.)*

RICHIE: *(Takes CHANCE's face in his hands.)* Who did this to you? *(CHANCE runs away. JOHNNY pulls him back onstage.)*

JULIA PASCAL

JOHNNY: It's fishing line. Look, the hook is still here.

RICHIE: *(Looking at his back.)* Hey!

JOHNNY: What?

RICHIE: The kid's been tortured. *(CHANCE pulls away.)*

JOEL: Let me see. *(JOEL looks.)* Give him back his T-shirt.

JOHNNY: Here you are, kid. *(CHANCE looks hostile.)*

JOHNNY: You don't want it? *(He taunts him with it and makes him jump.)*

RICHIE: Who hit you?

JOHNNY: Come here? *(Looks at his back.)*

JOHNNY: I won't hurt you. I just want to see. Someone worked hard on you. What did he want? *(CHANCE whimpers and runs away. They all look at him. CHANCE makes strange movements. It's a fish swallowing a man.)*

JOEL: Hanoj!

JOHNNY: Jonah? Jonah and the Whale? Is that what you're saying?

RICHIE: Jonah. Who is Jonah? You? Me? All of us? It makes no sense.

JOEL: A whale. We in a whale? Is that why it stinks?

JOHNNY: A friggin' whale?

RICHIE: Jonah got out.

JOEL: Hanoj?

JOHNNY: A whale? Is that what you're telling me? We're in a fucking whale?

JOEL: Whales talk don't they? They are smarter than us. Isn't that it?

JOHNNY: A fucking whale! With a clown, a stinking student, and a kid. What a lucky fucker am I!

RICHIE: *And Jonah was swallowed by a large fish.* In the Bible it doesn't say a whale.

JOHNNY: Whale or fish, what does it frigging matter?

RICHIE: A whale is a mammal. It's intelligent.

JOHNNY: And a fish is dumb? Yes this one's dumb. She got us.

RICHIE: If she's smart we can communicate with her.

JOHNNY: You speak whale now?

RICHIE: Think about it. Whale. What do they give us. Oil. Corset. Bones. Lamps. They're mammals. Like us. They got breasts.

JOEL: They got tits?

RICHIE: What is it with you?

JOEL: Maybe there is a reason/

JOHNNY: /we're in her belly?

RICHIE: We'll die here.

JOEL: Her belly? You think it's a girl, I know it's a girl. How do they make babies?

RICHIE: Sure it's a girl! Probably wearing a dress. It could fit your wife!

JOEL: I'll kill you.

RICHIE: Oh yeh!

JOHNNY: What about Sperm Whales? They're not girls.

RICHIE: Or killer whales. They eat other fish. That's it! We're in a killer whale. It's going eat us. We'll disappear. *(He laughs hysterically.)*

JOEL: I don't want to be in a whale. I want to be with my friends. I want to be there with them even if we have to.... don't make me.....why are you shaving your head and your beard and laughing because my chin is clean....don't make me do that.... *(Singing wildly.) Merrily merrily merrily merrily.*

(JOHNNY raises the steel pipe and threatens to hit him with it as he sings brutally.)

JOHNNY: *Life is but a dream. (Pause.)*

RICHIE: *(Beat.)* That smell.

JOHNNY: It's stomach juices.

JOEL: Bleach! ACID! Burns you up! *(Beat.)* What happened to Hanoj?

RICHIE: Jonah was a sinner. Like you.

JOHNNY: Did he knife a man in a ditch?

JOEL: What happened to him?

JOHNNY: He was vomited by the whale.

JOEL: Good.

JOHNNY: Why good?

JOEL: If she sicks up Jonah, then she'll sick us too.

JOHNNY: It's a story you cretin.

RICHIE: Poetry. Not reality! You don't believe all that!

JOEL: You mean it's not true?

JOHNNY: Sure it's true. The messiah will come and save us don't you know! *(Silence.)*

JOEL: If it's not true, then where are we? *(Screaming.)* Where are we? *(CHANCE covers his ears.)*

JOHNNY: Are you working? *(JOEL buckets.)*

JOEL: What did he have to do to get out? Hanoj?

JOHNNY: I told you it's made up!

RICHIE: It's poppycock.

JOEL: *(Learning the word.)* 'Poppy-cocky'.

<u>Movement scene:</u>

Another piece of steel is hurled in. Then more, and more. The stage becomes a kind of playground with the men playing violent games with the steel. The following speeches overlap.

JOHNNY: *(To JOEL.)* I could break your spine!

JOEL: I could smash your skull!

RICHIE: I could bore into your bowels. *(He stops as he remembers.)* Jonah, what do I know about Jonah/

JOEL: Be a man he says. I don't even have a moustache.

RICHIE: /he was to go to Nineveh to make the sinners stop.

JOEL: And that's why he was swallowed by a whale?

RICHIE: He had to make them repent/

JOEL: Did Jonah have a moustache?

RICHIE: /but he refused and *(JOEL picks up the steel pole.)*

RICHIE: Jonah ran away from God.

JOHNNY: *(Mocking.)* Hey God. Where are you?

JOEL: God! Look at us! Do you have ears God? Do you have a nose? *(JOEL stretches his hands up.)* Do you have a hand? *(Sound: Waves lapping.)*

RICHIE: I got it, I got it. Jonah fled God and got on a boat. Where was he? Jaffa? And God brought up a storm. And the sailors were frightened and they asked God to stop the storm. But God was deaf. So they begged him. And he said you have a man onboard who disobeys my orders. When you cast him off then the winds will stop. And the sailors said, no we can not throw a man into the icy sea to drown. And the storm got worse. Until Jonah said to the sailors, the man God is angry with, is me. I have ignored God's command. Save your lives. Throw me off the boat. Do it! And the sailors did. And the winds dropped. *(Silence.)*

JOEL: And the whale just happened to be passing by?

RICHIE: Don't be stupid!

JOEL: And it was yawning? Maybe it was tired. Do whales sleep?

RICHIE: Idiot!

JOEL: Do whales yawn? Does God? You think he gets bored or sleepy? If it's not a girl, if it's a Sperm Whale, does he have a wife?

JOHNNY: He shares her with you!

JOEL: Now I am going to kill you! *(JOEL makes a lunge at JOHNNY. RICHIE stops him)*

RICHIE: And the president of Africa asked God, *When will there be peace here?* And God said, *Mr President, not in your lifetime.* And the king of all of India asked God, *When will we have peace?* And God said, *Your royal lowness, not in your lifetime.* And the Chief of the Middle East asked God, *When will we have peace?* And God answered. *(Beat.) Not in my lifetime!*

JOHNNY: Let's get back to work.

JOEL: Why is there only one bucket?

JOHNNY: *(As if answering a joke.)* I don't know, why is there only one bucket?

RICHIE: I got it!

JOHNNY: What?

RICHIE: Jonah had to tell the people of Nineveh to repent and he refused.

JOHNNY: What?

RICHIE: So that's what we got to do.

JOEL: Repent. What's r-e-p-e-n-t?

JOHNNY: Repent having a fat wife. Repent not knowing Shakespeare. Repent killing a man in a ditch.

RICHIE: The kid's our repentance?

JOHNNY: What?

RICHIE: I don't know. Why's he here? Tell me that? Or maybe he's some kind of spy?

JOHNNY: Maybe that's it.

JOEL: Spy? Just look at him! *(They all look at him. He shrinks. Metal hinges are thrown onstage.)*

RICHIE: And who the hell is doing this? *(JOEL juggles with the pieces.)*

JOHNNY: What? *(CHANCE whimpers.)*

JOHNNY: What did you do?

RICHIE: What?

JOHNNY: To get here? You must have done something.

RICHIE: Nothing

JOEL: Yes you did. You sinned. Like Hanoj. You got thrown off the boat.

RICHIE: It wasn't Jonah that sinned. It was the people of Nineveh. *(JOEL grabs the book.)*

JOEL: The pages are stuck.

JOHNNY: Show me!

RICHIE: I kept it safe. From the water.

JOHNNY: Who glued it?

RICHIE: I got it that way.

JOEL: Here's a page with writing

JOHNNY: What can you read?

JOEL: The letter o. It's like a wide open mouth when you point the gun in. That's a double o. What don't they want you to read? *(RICHIE shrugs.)*

JOEL: Unstick it.

RICHIE: I can't

JOEL: Aren't you curious?

RICHIE: No. *(He violently beats the floor.)* How do we get out of here?

JOHNNY: We don't

JOEL: *(Hysterical.)* We going to die here? I don't want to die. Let me out.

(RICHIE hits JOEL and knocks him down.)

JOEL: You bastard. I've got a bullet/

JOHNNY: /in my ass. Did they get you in the balls too?

JOEL: Shut it!

JOHNNY: You need to work. We have to get out.

If that kid can get in then we can get out.

JOEL: We're getting out! Out!! Out!!!

(The following lines overlap. Each man is in his personal isolation but at moments he hears what the other says).

JOHNNY: I'm going home.

RICHIE: I'm going home.

JOHNNY: They'll all be waiting.

RICHIE: What will I tell him?

JOEL: Who?

RICHIE: About his girl?

JOEL: What girl?

JOHNNY: The place

JOEL: What?

JOHNNY: With the cement

JOEL: What cement? We're getting out

RICHIE: Out out out! He'll kill me!

JOEL: Who?

JOHNNY: I'll dig him up. And I'll see his green eyes

JOEL: I said who?

RICHIE: I'll build a school

JOEL: I'm going to play football for my country

JOHNNY: I'll find his mother

JOEL: Yes I am!

RICHIE: A school. For girls.

JOEL: Why for girls?

JOHNNY: and I'm going to build her a big house. You hear me?

JOEL: And the crowds will shout my name and they will see my face on a big TV but I have to keep my neck covered. They can't see my neck. And the blood when it pumps through, when I'm running and the veins stand out and the blood, don't let them see it.

RICHIE: Girls. And I'll teach them to fight...

JOEL: Girls will fight?

JOHNNY: The biggest house in the village made with bricks and wood no cement no cement no cement.

JOEL: and they will cheer and their sons will cheer and I will kick so high

JOHNNY: And when I walk through the town the people will look at me and on this day they'll say, this is the man that built the house for the woman whose son was buried alive in cement, why did he do that?

JOEL: that the ball will disappear into the clouds and nobody will see it and when it comes down it will be ten goals all at the same time.

JOHNNY: and then they'll guess and then they will come for me.

RICHIE: and they fight the men, they will kill the men who – no but I love you- why can't you look at me- look at me!!!

(Silence.)

CHANCE: *(Crying.)* Mother!

JOEL: *(Mocking.)* Mother!

JOHNNY: Shut it.

JOEL: Maybe I'll never see another woman in my whole life.

(Whale sound.)

JOEL: There was one once. I never told my wife.

RICHIE: Oh yes!

JOEL: It's true!

JOHNNY: Blind was she?

JOEL: I used to make her scream.

(JOHNNY covers his eyes. Looks at JOEL and screams.)

JOEL: Not like that.

JOHNNY: Really!

JOEL: Then she got tired of me.

RICHIE: You don't say.

JOEL: But why? When I made her come?

JOHNNY: Because you needed her.

Silence.

JOEL: What?

JOHNNY: Guy goes to a restaurant. Orders kebab. Eats kebab.
Tips the waitress. Next time he wants humus, tahini, felafel.
She's super-nice to him. Gives him extra felafel. This time
he leaves nothing. Has she done something wrong? Next
time he comes in. Orders a steak. Now he's spending a lot
of money. She's even keener to please. Will he? Won't he?
And so it goes on. One day he leaves silver on the table.
The next, nothing. She just can't work it out.

JOEL: So?

JOHNNY: That's how you keep a woman.

JOEL: Is it?

JOHNNY: And you never never never tell her you love her.

JOEL: But what if you do?

JOHNNY: That woman who screamed/

JOEL: /Yes?

JOHNNY: /that's what you told her?

JOEL: Yes.

JOHNNY: *(Opens his hands.)* You see!

JOEL: You're an animal. I bet you don't even love your
mother.

(JOHNNY attacks JOEL. It is brutal.)

JOHNNY: You dare to talk about my mother. I'll kill you. You
hear me!

(RICHIE pulls them apart. CHANCE watches.)

JOHNNY: You want to hear about her? My father was piss
poor. They got married. No money for a ring. He's
ashamed. What does he do? He saves up fifteen years to
buy her a diamond. He gives it to her and what does she
do? She throws it across the room. Not big enough. Not
good enough. Nothing is good enough for her. And my
father shitting his pants because she chucks it back in his
face. And you know what. Now that woman, she's old and
she's thin and she's alone and me what do I do? Do I have
to hate her even if she did throw back the diamond. Maybe
she hated him, maybe she hated him boring into her every
night and didn't want his stinking diamond and me I'm
stuck in this stinking fish with a load of stinking pigs.

Silence.

RICHIE: Did you ever tell your woman.......?

JOHNNY: About, about..?

RICHIE: What you did out there?

Did you, did you, I mean, you know, did you tell, I mean
tell her, I mean what you did, I mean, when you were
away, I mean when you were with the men/

JOHNNY: /No.

RICHIE: Me neither. I just, I just/

JOHNNY: /A woman can't …….. She can't/

RICHIE: No. She wouldn't

JOHNNY: /understand

RICHIE: /understand, that's right.

JOEL: Tell what? Tell what? Tell what?

JOHNNY: You tell your fat wife about the man in the ditch? Do
you?

*(JOEL is disturbed. He looks for CHANCE and tries to hold him.
CHANCE runs away.)*

Silence.

RICHIE: *(In his head to the woman we learn he has later killed.)*
    Why don't you love me?

JOHNNY: Love! How does it end up? Look at us. Born
    between piss and shit.

JOEL: What?

JOHNNY: It's only slime.

RICHIE: Slime?

JOHNNY: Hers?

JOEL: And yours

JOHNNY: She's got blood too.

JOEL: Slime is all we are. Like this fish.

RICHIE: Don't say that. She's my diamond

    (CHANCE looks up at the word diamond.)

    (Memory.) Look at me!

JOHNNY: You never thought it? *(Beat.)* When you touch a
    woman? You want her but you hate her. For making you.
    Want her?

RICHIE: It's not like that for me.

JOHNNY: What is it then? *(RICHIE covers his ears.)*

    What did you do?

RICHIE: Nothing.

JOHNNY: That's not true.

JOEL: What? *(Beat.)* You did something to a woman? You
    did, didn't you. I know you did. I can feel it. Something
    terrible. You're like him. Just the same. Cold. No heart.
    And a coward. It's true. Behind all your clever books and
    your talk you're scared, like that kid!

    *(RICHIE goes to attack JOEL. RICHIE beats him and we should
    think he will kill him. RICHIE then holds JOEL who goes floppy
    like a rag doll.)*

RICHIE: Look at me! Look at me! Look at me! Look at me!
    Look at me! Look at me! Look at me! Look at me! Look

at me! Look at me! Look at me! Look at me!Look at me!
Look at me! Look at me! Look at me!

JOHNNY: Who you talking to?

(JOEL wails)

(RICHIE drops him.)

JOHNNY: Who? Who? Who?

RICHIE: I said shut up.

(This to JOEL but he is talking to someone else)

Look at me!

I know you are my brother's girl but I want you. Look at
me. Why don't you look? I bring you food. And water. I sit
with you here in the hut. Fourteen days and fifteen nights
and you won't look at me. What have I done to you?
Nothing. You don't love him. You love me. Say it. Say it?

(He hits JOEL.)

You smell good to me. You don't wash and you smell good.
You're mine. You hear me. You're too good for him. Me.
That's who you need. I'm a good man. Tell me I'm a good
man. *(He 'rapes' her again and again.)* Look at me. Look at
me girl. If you don't I don't know what I'll do. Look at
me! Or I will have to do something so that you never see
him again, if I can't have you then he will never and it's
because I love you that I have to do this

I have to... I have... I, I, I.......

(JOEL yells as if he has become the 'girl'. He breaks free angrily.)

*(RICHIE picks up his book. He tries to unglue it. Failing he throws it
on the ground in rage. JOEL goes up to him and puts his arm around
him. RICHIE throws him off violently.)*

Silence.

SOUND of water.

*(RICHIE waves his book in the air as if to oppose somebody (God?)
and slowly lets it drop to the ground.)*

(JOEL sings 'Row Your Boat' fast and then gradually it slows as if an old-fashioned record on a gramophone has run down.)

BLACKOUT

LIGHTS UP

RICHIE: Nobody will remember our names.

JOHNNY: What?

RICHIE: We'll get swallowed up here and disappear. Because we sinned

JOEL: We didn't sin. Did we? Did we? The man in the ditch? With the knife. And his neck? But they made me!

JOHNNY: It's war. It isn't our fault

RICHIE: *(Mocking.)* It isn't our fault! It isn't our fault!

Pause.

JOEL: Unstick the book. Maybe there's a message.

RICHIE: Yes. A message from the prophet Elijah. Or Jeremiah!

JOEL: Don't be silly. From Jonah.

(RICHIE and JOHNNY laugh.)

JOEL: Did Jonah have a son? *(Beat.)* I want one.

RICHIE: You? A son with who? The whale. You want to fuck the whale?

JOEL: I hate you.

RICHIE: You want one?

JOEL: Your own boy? Teach him to fight?

JOHNNY: Shut it.

JOEL: What?

JOHNNY: Go to hell.

JOEL: You have a child?

JOHNNY: I said shut it.

JOEL: You do! You do!

JOHNNY goes to hit him. RICHIE stops him.

JOHNNY: You want to know, you want to know, cretin? I saw him born!

JOEL: What?

RICHIE: Who's the woman?

JOHNNY: My son, like a small animal. At her breasts. His mouth. Milk. Thick like cement. And he. The man. My son's eyes. Green. Just like the man's. Who is sucking? The boy? The man? The man whose eyes are staring. Screaming. With the cement. The milky cement and he is screaming mother only he is a baby he can't say mother. Shut up! And shut up shut up shut up!

(CHANCE walks across the stage. JOHNNY looks at him.)

(RICHIE and JOEL exchange looks. There is a connection. They turn to JOHNNY)

RICHIE: It's alright now.

JOHNNY: Nothing's all right. Not after I, after I, after. Nothing will ever be right ever again.

(RICHIE and JOEL look at one another)

<u>*Movement scene:*</u>

The whale jumps. They jump too.

(SOUND of large explosion. Everyone is jumping. The stage is full of their activity. It's like a grenade or is it a game?)

(More debris has littered the stage and the planking is everywhere)

(JOHNNY takes a plank. He picks up steel poles. He wheels it around as if it is a weapon. He turns against the others.

CHANCE takes the poles and starts to assemble the scaffolding. The others watch.)

RICHIE: The kid. He's built stuff.

JOEL: I can build too.

RICHIE: You?

JOEL: I wanted to be a farmer before they took me to the army. Cows and sheep. Grow my own vegetables. Calm.

(CHANCE continues to assemble the material.

JOEL applauds. CHANCE turns slowly.

At first he is frightened then he realises this is acclaim.)

RICHIE: We need more planks to get out of here.

JOEL: We can get out?

RICHIE: Hey, let's do it! A tower. We'll make a tower! There must be a way. We don't have to die!

JOEL: Like Babel! You think we can get out? Or maybe through the arse? Shat from a whale's arse? Do they have arses? Yes! Everything does. Does God?

SOUND of water.

RICHIE: Something's wrong.

JOEL: What?

RICHIE: There's something missing.

JOEL: If I was a farmer I would have a barn. We could hide. In the hay. Under the belly of the cow. Make ourselves small and curl into the sheep's fleece.

RICHIE: You and the kid could hide. You're boys.

JOEL: If there are no sheep, dig a hole. Sleep in the soil.

JOHNNY: Dig a hole. Sleep in the soil. No!

(As if someone is saying this to him. This is a new voice)

You. Dig a hole! Move it! You run and you let the others do the dirty work. Your brother. Look! They cut off his nose. His ears. And they make him naked. And then they cut! Cut the man off him and the blood filling the earth. You going to let the man go who did that? Are you?

(He stands frozen).

(JOHNNY does training exercises with a gun (pole). Star jumps. Running on the spot with knees up to his chest. He speaks and trains at the same time so that the following monologue makes him breathless and is not fluent).

JOHNNY: *(Memory.)*

But I can't.

(As if someone else giving orders).

Dig!

(He 'digs' with a steel pole).

(As if someone else giving orders).

Throw him in the hole!

(As if someone else giving orders).

Bring in the cement!

I can't!

(As if someone else giving orders).

Do it! *(He laughs).*

(As if someone else giving orders).

Why are you laughing? Do it!

(As if someone else giving orders).

STOP LAUGHING!

(He freezes. Unfreezes and then we realise he is carrying out the orders.)

JOHNNY: *(His text is intercut with his hysterical laugh. The effect is jagged and disturbing).* Hey you! I know you! My brother! You remember what you do to him?

You like to dance. Hot isn't it. Go on driver, fill the hole up to his waist-you not dancing now. Up to the neck in the mouth and then your eyes, greenest green with the white of the cement in your mouth and the green of your eyes and my whole head is green and green

Mother help me I don't want to die!

Silence.

JOEL: You're right,

RICHIE: What?

JOEL: My mother never knew my father.

RICHIE: What?

JOEL: And my wife is fat. She makes cakes. I tell her stop with the baking but she can't.

RICHIE: Why can't we get out of here. What is it that's missing? *(Beat.)* We haven't all talked!

JOEL: We haven't all talked! We haven't all talked!

JOHNNY: The kid's not talking.

RICHIE: Well he can't.

JOEL: So according to your theory, if we all talk, out we go?

RICHIE: It's a hunch.

JOEL: But this tower stuff, it's all cocky-poppy. I know. This whale. She's got holes on the top of her head. Blow holes. One or two. We could climb out! Jump out.

CHANCE comes up to them with a leaf.

RICHIE: What's he telling us?

JOEL: We're near land!

CHANCE rips out the stitches.

(SOUND of guns in the distance)

CHANCE: Die- A- Monds.

JOEL: What?

CHANCE: My uncle/

RICHIE: What?

CHANCE: /his stomach big swelling he's sick and they think he has diamonds so they cut him open…

JOHNNY: Come on!

CHANCE: I go to the tap. With the kids and the wives. Fill the bucket. Wash. Then school. Bang! The rebels are coming. But I have to fill the bucket. What will they say if I come home and the bucket is empty? And I run and the house is empty. And the rebels are coming. They want the diamonds. They want me. And I jump to my neighbour's house and I hide in the wall. And they scream *Where is he?* and they beat the neighbour until he is screaming no more and his wife is screaming no more, what can I do, if I come I am dead and my heart beats in my ears so loud they will hear it and take me and I run back to the house and they find me and they make me carry their guns and if I run I am dead

RICHIE, JOHNNY and JOEL overlap.

RICHIE: What did you do kid?

JOHNNY: What did you do?

JOEL: We'll never get out. I'll never learn to read properly. I'm going to die here. With the stink. With the water. His blood in my mouth down my lungs and waves and waves of it inside me.

(During the past few minutes CHANCE has been constructing the scaffolding)

RICHIE: He's at least doing something.

JOEL: Stupid! We'll die here and it's all your fault. You could do something and all you do is read your cretin book.

(JOEL grabs it. They fight. JOEL gets it JOEL goes to the glued pages.)

JOEL: You want to read this? Do you? You know what's in it? Open it. I dare you!

(RICHIE remains inert.)

Silence.

SOUND of a high wind.

CHANCE takes the book from JOEL.

He unglues the pages.

RICHIE: What does it say?

JOHNNY: *(Takes it from him.)* Men

RICHIE: What about them?

JOHNNY: Women-children. They got faces like yours. How is that?

RICHIE: I don't want to hear.

JOHNNY: In pits. Thousands and thousands of them shovelled into the ground-so-full it's moving with the dead. Dead people and they're all carrying books. And kissing them.

RICHIE: Shut it!

JOHNNY: And coming to the moving soil and the moving people and the men *(Beat.)* soldiers

RICHIE: What soldiers?

JOHNNY: They are being sick. Sick from what they see. Skeletons kissing books!

RICHIE: *(Shouting.)* Why was it glued?

JOHNNY: And the dead rise up.

RICHIE: *(As if he is now telling the story. As if he understands it through touch/reading with his fingers.)* Want to kill.

JOHNNY: The dead want to kill?

RICHIE: Kill the satan-men who killed them. But they can't find them. They all ran away. Those devils, they hid what they did.

JOEL: So the dead, they find others and they kill them instead. So angry they have to kill somebody.

JOHNNY: And then it's done.

RICHIE: And the children of the new dead, they seal the books because they want to hide what happened to the men and women in the pits[1]. They seal the books. The books that used to be kissed.

JOEL: *(Clowning and jumping up and down as if being blown to bits in a grenade attack.)*
And so it goes on
And so it goes on

---

1 This passage is an allusion to soldiers liberating Belsen. The dead people carrying books are a reference to The People Of The Book-Jews. The image of the glued book comes from Conant's research in Lebanon. There she saw children's history books where chapters on The Holocaust were glued shut.

And so it goes on
And so it goes on

SPOT on CHANCE.

CHANCE: And they put the long cold steel in my hands and
they scream at me

Kill your mother!

Kill your father!

Mother! Father! Your mouths are two rounds like two
empty cooking pots

*(He falls to the floor as if hit. When he speaks, it is the man's voice
that is in his memory.)*

CHANCE: Do it or we kill you!

Mother! Your eyes, swimming all over your face. Father!
You give me the money to go to school. And I don't spill
the water. I come back. The tap so high I have to reach
and reach. And when I come back with the bucket, the
plates are on the table but the wives and the children are
gone. Father, don't look at the ground. Why does the man
with the gun smell so bad?

(Memory. He is hit on the back.)

Ow!

(His mother's voice in his head.)

Do it son! Do whatever he wants. It doesn't matter if we
die. You must live!

Run! I have to run away. But mother. I can't leave you.
Father I can't leave you.

(He slows down.)

(Man's voice from inside him.)

Come on boy. Drink this.

It smells bad like the man. Like the men who come for me.
(Swallows.)

It's fire!

(Man's voice from inside him.)

Drink boy, drink boy, you come with us.

(Silence as his breath is very fast.)

Mother!

Mother!!

I can't leave you!!!

(Man's voice from inside him)

Drink boy, drink a lot!

(Mother's voice.)

Do what they tell you son.*(Beat.)*

(Man's voice from inside him)

Come with me boy.

(CHANCE picks up a steel bar as if it is a gun.)

(Man's voice from inside him)

Take it boy. Don't be scared. Take it. It won't hurt you. It feels good, doesn't it. Your hand on the trigger.

You have to look. Close one eye. See your enemy better. Make him disappear. Then you will be one of us.

We will look after you. You'll like it with us. With the other boys. We have big cars. We have diamonds. We have planes and guns. You like that.

And when you get big down here you have girls. You know you want to be one of us.

Come on boy. Come on boy! Time to be a man! Hit her!

I want to run. If I run I die!

(Man's voice from inside him.)

Show us you're a man.

She's my mother!

(Man's voice from inside him.)

Go on boy!

No!

(Man's voice from inside him.)

You stamp on her chest.

No!

(Mother's voice)

Do it son! Do it!

RICKIE: ECNAHC

CHANCE: My name. Chance.

JOHNNY: Chance.

RICKIE: Chance means luck.

JOEL: You can be our good luck!

CHANCE: What's that?

JOHNNY: Luck! Look at him. He killed his own mother!

(CHANCE howls.)

RICHIE: We're all killers.

JOHNNY: We didn't do that though.

(To RICHIE.) Did you kill your mother?

(To JOEL.) Or you?

SOUND *of guns in the distance.*

JOEL: What do we do?

JOHNNY: We stay.

JOEL: We go.

RICHIE: Johnny?

JOHNNY: Oh let's follow Shakespeare! He can't even read.

RICHIE: Maybe he's right

JOHNNY: Right?

RICHIE: What is there to lose?

JOHNNY: Lose? Nothing! *(Beat.)*

Suppose you get out. Listen to what's going on out there. The rebel army. Make you a killer again. You want that?

RICHIE: I am a killer.

JOHNNY: Are you? Are you really? Deep down?

RICHIE: Aren't you?

JOHNNY: Get out of here! Go with the cretin and the kid.

JOEL takes off his watch. Offers it to CHANCE.

JOEL: Here, kid. This has diamonds. You want it?

Silence.

CHANCE slowly takes the watch. He looks at it and throws it.

CHANCE: Diamonds kill my mother.

Silence.

JOHNNY grabs CHANCE.

JOHNNY: Who the hell sent you?

JOEL: Nobody sent him!

RICHIE: How can we trust a kid who kills his mother. And the lips. It was you that sewed them!

JOHNNY: Hey Mr-what-are-you? You sent by the rebels. That's the truth isn't it.

RICHIE: You need men. Like us. Men to get diamonds.

JOHNNY: Diamonds. Smart cars. That's why you build all this.

RICHIE: He kills his mother! Kills his mother! I never kill my mother. Did I kill my mother? Did I kill a woman? Did I? Did I? A woman? Kill her? Did I?

JOEL: Stop! You going to kill him!

JOHNNY: Kill a killer! A man who murders the woman who gave him life!

JOEL: You'll be punished!

JOHNNY: Oh yeh? By who? We're in a whale!

JOEL: When we get out.

JOHNNY: Get out! And if we do? Who knows about all this? Who gives a shit!

CHANCE: The sun is dreaming. There is quiet in the village. I see smoke.I am your boy. I have to come back.Mother, why is your bright yellow dress around your neck?

JOEL: We don't deserve it

JOHNNY: What?

JOEL: To get out. I stink. We all do.

JOHNNY: Go to hell. Both of you. To hell with you and the boy who kills his mother!

RICHIE: We're not as bad as him

JOEL: We can try again

JOHNNY: Try again? *(Facetiously.)* You do that! Only promise me one thing?

JOEL: What?

JOHNNY: If you get out,

JOEL: If we get out?

JOHNNY: Which you won't. But if you do.

JOEL: What?

JOHNNY: You never. Never. Never. Say my name.

RICHIE: What is your name? Johnny What?

JOHNNY: Johnny Nobody. Johnny. Nothing.

RICHIE: Nothing.

JOEL: You can't stop me talking. You can't!

RICHIE: Come with us.

Silence.

(Huge tension between RICHIE and JOHNNY)

JOHNNY: Get out

JOEL reaches out his hand to JOHNNY.

JOHNNY hits him, JOEL is hurt.

CHANCE starts to climb the structure.

JOEL: I follow the kid. Who is coming with me?

CHANCE: You help me read?

JOEL: Me?

CHANCE: You? *(Looking at RICHIE.)* And you?

JOEL: Why you want to read?

CHANCE: I want to go back home. When I can read.

JOEL: What for?

CHANCE: You laugh.

RICHIE: No.

CHANCE: Some day I tell you.

JOEL: Now!

CHANCE: No!

RICHIE: Come on!

JOEL: I want. I can. Be someone…

JOEL: Who?

CHANCE: but only if I can read

RICHIE: Who?

CHANCE: like people who write books. Like you!

RICHIE: Who?

CHANCE: No. I can't.

Pause.

RICHIE: I've got to know!

CHANCE: No!

RICHIE: I won't laugh

CHANCE: My country. One day.

RICHIE: Yes?

CHANCE: But only when I can read.

RICHIE: Yes?

CHANCE: *(Beat.)* The president.

> *SOUND OF THE WATER AND THE GUNS.*

RICHIE: You?

CHANCE: Me.

RICHIE: The President? The President? *(Beat.)* Why not.

> *(A look between JOEL and RICHIE which connects them to CHANCE.)*

JOEL: Let's go. Mister President.

CHANCE: You laughing at me!

JOEL: No I am not.

CHANCE: Give me the book.

> *Pause.*

> *RICHIE gives it to him.*

> *CHANCE kisses it and puts it over his heart.*

> *JOEL looks at RICHIE. He is convinced by CHANCE. RICHIE is touched by CHANCE's love of the book.*

RICHIE: Johnny. You coming?

> *JOHNNY ignores him.*

> *CHANCE climbs and reaches out to JOEL.*

> *JOEL takes his hand.*

> *CHANCE climbs with the book held high to keep it safe.*

> *JOEL follows him and RICHIE makes reluctant steps to follow.*

> *JOHNNY remains. He holds an empty bucket to his chest and keens with it silently.*

> *Slow fade to blackout. The sound of the guns mixes with the sound of children's voices in the distance. Frozen image of the three men climbing with the book held at the highest point. JOHNNY is turned away from them.*

ENDS

WOMAN ON THE BRIDGE

Woman On The Bridge is dedicated to Evelyn and Rachel Waldstein.

Public readings of *Woman On The Bridge.*

New York City 14 October 2013.
Cast: Kristen Doscher, Barbara Haas, Frank de Julio,
Romy Nordlinger, Andrea J. Nouryeh, Maria Pastel, Brian
Richardson. Directed by Ludovica Villar-Hauser.
This was part of the Young Blood Season at Theater for the
New City.

15 October.

It was also read at Julia's Reading Room for LPTW.

London
20 January 2012, NYU in London.
Cast: Amanda Boxer, Valerie Cutko, Alex Guiney, Ruth
Posner, Anna Savva, Stephanie Street.
This reading was organised as part of The League of
Professional Women's 30 Plays Season.

London

9 November 2009, The Drill Hall.
Cast: Fiz Marcus, Matthew Naegli, Diana Payan, Ruth
Posner, Anna Savva, Jennifer Ward.

Both London readings directed by Julia Pascal.

The author would like to thank Andrea J. Nouryeh, Ph.D.
for dramaturgy on these texts, Dr Geraldine Cohen for
editing and David Schneider for assistance with Yiddish
terms.

Characters

JUDITH GREEN
A BBC radio journalist. She is slim. (55)

ANDY VOGEL
A New York actor. German parents. (23)

GLORIA SANCHEZ-RYAN
New York Police Department cop. Born in NYC
of Puerto Rican parents. Married to an Irishman.
(44)

SUSAN PETERS
New Yorker. (23)

LOUISE WACHMAN
Polish Jew. Holocaust survivor. (80)

ANNA WEIB
Left Romania after WW2. New Yorker. Judith's
great aunt. (110)

Hospital Worker

Joggers

Skateboarder

Voices off

With doubling the play can be done with 5-7 actors.

LOCATIONS

JFK Airport

A hotel bedroom in Manhattan

The New York Subway

An apartment mid-town Manhattan

Brooklyn Bridge

SCENE ONE

Inside of a jet that has just flown from London to John F. Kennedy. This is in blackout as lights are coming up slowly. Voices 1-4 are middle-class English women.

V/O (NEW YORK AIR HOSTESS): Please keep your seat belts fastened until the aircraft comes to a complete stop.

(Sound. From the interior of the plane. The sound of the steps arriving outside and the doors opening.)

V/O (MALE PILOT. AMERICAN): Ladies and gentlemen. Welcome to JFK where the local time is seven pm. On behalf of Captain Frank Ulysses and his team, we hope you had a pleasant flight, we appreciate your business and look forward to seeing you again on American Airlines.

(Spotlight on JUDITH - Inside JFK Airport. She is disorientated and lost in the soundscape.)

(These voices are shouted at the lines of people waiting to pass the entry lines.)

V/O (1): Line 25! Over here!

V/O (2): Passports open at the photo page!

V/O (3): Move it!

V/O (4): Line 30!

(During the following dialogue her phone is ringing and she picks it out of her bag, looks at the screen and refuses the call.

(Sound mix of different accents and voices in the airport as people are milling around and getting into lines.)

(VOICES 1-4 are middle class young English women.)

VOICE 1: Where do we queue?

VOICE 2: Down the hall?

VOICE 3: Is there a toilet here? I didn't go on the plane.

VOICE 4: Don't say toilet say restroom/

VOICE 3: A whole seven hours and I'm dying but, if the plane crashes, and I'm caught with my knickers down…!

VOICE 4: /or bathroom.

(JUDITH's phone is ringing again. This time she answers.)

JUDITH: Stop calling me. Just stop.

IMMIGRATION OFFICER: *(Yelling.)* Lady. Over there. Line number five.

(JUDITH is carrying a small bag and a laptop in a shoulder bag as well as newspapers and her immigration papers. She puts her index finger out for finger printing at immigration.)

V/O: You here to work Miss?

JUDITH: I'm here to see Manhattan.

V/O: Vacation or business?

JUDITH: Sorry?

V/O: *(Irritated.)* I said vacation or business?

JUDITH: To see the Brooklyn Bridge.

V/O: Miss! Look straight at the camera. *(Beat.)* And again. Straight!

(JUDITH looks straight out.)

V/O: OK. Next. *(JUDITH doesn't move.)* I said next!

(Cross fade into Scene Two.)

SCENE TWO

A hotel room in Manhattan. East 79th Street.

Sounds of police sirens. (The point of view is JUDITH's. She is in a hotel and the sounds are out in the street. The windows are open. She is on the 12th floor). Sounds of traffic. JUDITH calls. Her phone is on speaker. She does not have it in her hand.

JUDITH: Hey Diane, sorry you're not there. What time is it in London? I'm in the hotel.

(JUDITH opens her case and takes out clothes. She throws them on the bed wildly. She puts on a dress. It is back to front. She groans with rage.)

Stupid bitch! *(JUDITH slaps her face. She tries to get the dress on right but the logic of it defeats her.)*

(A phone rings. It is her London phone.)

JUDITH: No! No! No!

(She throws it on the bed. She returns to the speaker)

Diane he's calling me all the time. I can't. I just can't.

(She rummages among her clothes and papers)

Somewhere there is a map. I can't get this place, it's all straight lines, avenues-streets, up and down and then suddenly it's all letters Bleeker and Bleeker. If I understand the underground then I'll be alright. All right. Right. Right. Right.

(Sound of sirens.)

(In total frustration JUDITH turns on the remote for the TV. She tries to fold her clothes into neat piles and is not successful. The programme is Reality TV.)

PRESENTER: ...and you, Patrick, you say that Darren, Felicia's child, this three-year-old boy, is not yours. Is that true?

PATRICK: That kid doesn't even look like me.

FELICIA: He's lying. He's got a new girlfriend and she's put him up to it.

CARA: That's not true. The bitch wants to get his money, to pay for her and her kids but he's my fiancé. He's going to be my husband.

PRESENTER: And see you after the break.

(Sound of romantic music.)

MALE V/O: Hey guys! Are you worried about your performance? This may be the answer to your dreams.

(More romantic music.)

MALE V/O: If you want to please the woman in your life, and give her the greatest pleasure in the world, Prialis is for you.

(Her mobile phone rings. She looks at the number and cancels the call.)

MALE V/O: But if you have any of the following conditions consult your doctor first.

(More romantic music.)

(Her mobile phone rings again. She yells at it.)

JUDITH: Yes Peter. I'm in New York. Leave me alone can't you?

MALE V/O: Palpitations or any uneven heartbeat…

(Romantic music is still playing.)

MALE V/O: Chest pain, changes of vision, shortness of breath, constant erection.

(Her phone rings.)

JUDITH: No!

(She answers it.)

I've nothing to say to you. (……)

What do you want of me Peter? (…)

It's over. I told you. I'm through. (……)

What? Well you can't

(Hangs up.)

(Phone rings again.)

JUDITH: Will you stop calling me.

(Hangs up.)

(It rings again.)

JUDITH: I'm crazy? You fuck your mother's maid and I'm crazy?

Not the maid. What is she? Oh the carer. She certainly cares about your marriage!

(Hangs up. Packs. Phone rings again.)

(Beat.) You and me? In fifteen years, it was never just you and me.

I'm getting out of here. *(…)*

Anywhere you can't find me. *(…)*

What for? It's over. You killed it. *(….)*

At least you're alive! What does that mean? Nothing? So go. Be alive. Live with her. *(….)*

You can't leave me? You can't leave her and you can't leave me. Did you become a Muslim? I'm out of this. You hear me? OUT.

(She hangs up.)

(Her mobile phone rings again. She throws it on the bed. A moment later JUDITH takes a newspaper and beats a chair with it. She is sobbing with fury.)

PRESENTER: And, after that short break welcome back to *Whose Baby Is It?*

Now Patrick and Felicia. Stop fighting and calm it will you?

PATRICK: Felicia's a slut. A whore. She's done it with everyone. She can't prove that's my kid.

PRESENTER: I have the DNA test here and, now Patrick, if it's positive will you support the child?

CARA: It's not true. She wants to steal him back.

FELICIA: You bitch, you stole him with your fat tits and your fat ass

PRESENTER: Now ladies stop fighting. Here is the evidence. *(Music.)*

And the answer is… *(Drumbeat.)* Patrick….the DNA proves that Darren is *(Drumbeat intensifies to a climax.)* … your child!

(Uproar from the crowd.)

(Uproar broken by the sound of a whistle from a doorman hailing a cab in the street which changes the scene.)

(Cross fade.)

SCENE THREE

In the Subway.

(JUDITH is standing on the subway platform. A train is coming. She breathes in as it comes closer. She has an impulse to jump in front of it. The train pulls in. She breathes out.)

SCENE FOUR

JUDITH's hotel bedroom. New York.

Upper East Side. East 79th Street.

(JUDITH is in bed with ANDY.)

ANDY: Sorry.

JUDITH: It's OK.

ANDY: I'm never so quick.

JUDITH: It's OK.

ANDY: You got me going.

JUDITH: Yes.

ANDY: Maybe later.

JUDITH: Yes.

ANDY: It's stress.

JUDITH: Don't worry.

ANDY: I always worry. *(Beat.)* Why did you lie?

JUDITH: When?

ANDY: Online.

JUDITH: What?

ANDY: You said you're old.

JUDITH: You're sweet.

ANDY: You're like a girl.

JUDITH: *(Wryly.)* That's right.

ANDY: You know you should be careful.

JUDITH: That's not an issue.

ANDY: What?

JUDITH: It's unlikely.

ANDY: What?

JUDITH: Oh. Nothing.

ANDY: You don't even know who I am.

JUDITH: You're OK.

ANDY: I could be a murderer. Strangle you with a sheet. Nobody would know.

JUDITH: One schmuck less in the world. *(Beat.)* You want to sleep?

ANDY: What's your name?

JUDITH: I told you.

ANDY: Angela*? (Shaking his head.)* Uh huh.

JUDITH: Why not?

ANDY: Angela is blonde with a snub nose.

JUDITH: Tonight that's who I am.

ANDY: I'm Andreas.

JUDITH: *(Holding out her hand in mock courtesy.)* How do you do!

ANDY: Everyone calls me Andy.

JUDITH: So we both have names beginning with A.

ANDY: And yours is?

JUDITH: Anon. I wrote a lot poetry. *(She looks at him for a response.)* Never mind.

ANDY: Gertrude!

JUDITH: *(Laughing.)* Gertrude!

ANDY: Cleopatra?

JUDITH: I love it!

ANDY: Ophelia?

JUDITH: Oh-feel-iya.

ANDY: Eurydice?

JUDITH: Well, you're either an actor or a singer?

ANDY: How did you guess? *(She shrugs.)* What's your work?

JUDITH: You know.

ANDY: No.

JUDITH: People.

ANDY: You don't give much away.

JUDITH: Coming out of the lift, sorry elevator, did you see that cute marmalade cat?/

ANDY: /Why won't you tell me?/

JUDITH: /Yesterday I tried to get him to come in but he was shy. All orange cats are male, did you know that?

ANDY: I like cats too. And dogs. 'Angela'!

JUDITH: *(Stretching.)* Do I want to sleep or eat?

ANDY: First a nap and then we'll go out.

JUDITH: No. We won't.

ANDY: Mm?

JUDITH: Go out.

ANDY: What?

JUDITH: I don't date.

ANDY: You don't date?

JUDITH: I'm a married woman.

ANDY: Oh.

JUDITH: Does that bother you?

ANDY: I thought you were...

JUDITH: What?

ANDY: ...maybe divorced.

JUDITH: Why?

ANDY: No ring.

JUDITH: It pinches.

ANDY: Someone's wife. Je-e-s-u-s.

JUDITH: And that's a problem?

ANDY: Where is he? Your husband.

JUDITH: What time is it in Europe?

ANDY: Seven.

JUDITH: Probably having dinner with another woman.

ANDY: Oh.

JUDITH: OK. For you, I break the rules. Let's go out.

ANDY: You should be with him.

JUDITH: Maybe he should be with me.

ANDY: You're smart. I like that.

JUDITH: There's a diner on Madison does great omelettes. I'm sure it's still open.

ANDY: Marriage is marriage.

JUDITH: You're very old for a young man.

ANDY: How old?

JUDITH: Five thousand and something. What are you? Catholic?

ANDY: Maybe.

JUDITH: And you believe?

ANDY: I'm Bavarian.

JUDITH: Ah yes. Andreas. Why have you no accent?

ANDY: *(In stage German.)* Vot du you vant me to talk like in der cinema?

JUDITH: Ja! Bestimmt. *(German for 'Yes! Exactly.')*

ANDY: My parents came to New York when I was a kid. They always say Bavaria is not Germany.

JUDITH: Meaning?

ANDY: I don't know. More Latin. More Italian. Hell I'm tired.

JUDITH: Yes sleep. That's what men do. It's chemical.

ANDY: Was it enough?

JUDITH: What?

ANDY: My dick.

JUDITH: What?

ANDY: I know I was too fast but it's always like that the first time.

JUDITH: No angst.

ANDY: But I mean even if it's not that long, the width, that's what counts isn't it. That's what women tell me.

JUDITH: Oh you don't need to worry. *(He sleeps and then jerks awake.)*

ANDY: Did I sleep?

JUDITH: One whole second.

ANDY: What time is it?

JUDITH: Midnight.

ANDY: And tomorrow morning I've got to get this audition or I'm dead.

JUDITH: What is it?

ANDY: Ten of us for one role. My first Broadway break. Hey, why don't you meet me afterwards? Give me something else to think about.

JUDITH: I'll call you.

ANDY: You don't have my number.

JUDITH: I'll take it.

ANDY: What's yours?

JUDITH: I've no cell.

ANDY: I don't believe you.

JUDITH: If I want you I'll find you.

ANDY: Do you know how many cute young men there are in Manhattan. They'll all be hitting on you. You'll forget me.

JUDITH: You're crazy!

ANDY: If I don't get this part, I could come to London. See you there. Would you like that?

JUDITH: When I was thirty you were born.

ANDY: I don't care.

JUDITH: Why you interested in someone my age?

ANDY: You're pretty. You're soft.

JUDITH: And that's all there is to it?

ANDY: You're a woman.

JUDITH: I like that.

(He changes position.)

ANDY: You shouldn't deceive your husband.

(JUDITH laughs.)

It's not right.

JUDITH: You are joking.

ANDY: I mean it.

JUDITH: If it bugs you why do you want to come to London to see me?

ANDY: I don't know.

JUDITH: Why don't you date women your age?

ANDY: They want money. They want a husband. Not actors who wait tables.

(Silence.)

They get to thirty they want a baby. You had babies?

JUDITH: No.

ANDY: Did you want them?

JUDITH: I had a shit mother. Repetition's not my thing.

ANDY: Your mom? What was her problem?

JUDITH: She wanted to be the only girl in the/

ANDY: /We could have a girl/

JUDITH: /world and gave me away. To her mother./

ANDY: /My looks. Your cute ass!

(JUDITH laughs. ANDY looks awkward and then joins in.)

ANDY: Tell me something.

JUDITH: What?

ANDY: About the old lady brought you up. Your grandmother.

JUDITH: The only person who ever loved me.

ANDY: Why wouldn't she love you?

JUDITH: But she never said it.

ANDY: What else?

JUDITH: She had a funny accent. Foreign. Almost German.

ANDY: Tell me something secret. About her.

JUDITH: When I was fourteen. I found *The Marquis de Sade* hidden under tea cloths in the sideboard. Old people thinking about sex! Yuk! *(Moving to get up.)* I need to eat.

ANDY: *(Holding her back.)* Tell me.

JUDITH: Tell you what?

ANDY: A story from your life.

JUDITH: What do you want from me Andreas? I've nothing to give you.

ANDY: Distract me.

JUDITH: From what?

ANDY: I am frightened of tomorrow. I don't want to think about it.

JUDITH: OK.

ANDY: Go on.

JUDITH: When I was forty, I met this man.

ANDY: Who? This husband?

JUDITH: Then he was someone else's. *(Beat.)* I can't do this.

ANDY: OK.

JUDITH: I have to get out of here.

ANDY: Your first kiss.

JUDITH: OK.

ANDY: How old are you?

JUDITH: Twelve.

ANDY: Twelve.

JUDITH: Mature kid.

ANDY: Who is he?

JUDITH: A friend of my brother's. Tall, blond, with a long nose.

ANDY: Tell me.

JUDITH: It's at a party. Everyone is a teenager. And can you believe, I'm just a kid in white ankle socks! He's sixteen.

ANDY: Go on.

JUDITH: It's summer. All the other girls are in nylon stockings. They've got such big legs!

ANDY: Where are you?

JUDITH: A trashy seaside town in the north of England. We're in the smart area.

ANDY: Name?

JUDITH: You wouldn't know.

ANDY: Name!

JUDITH: Southport. Ever heard of it?

ANDY: No. *(Beat.)* What does he do to you?

JUDITH: Pulls me onto his knee.

ANDY: What's his name?

JUDITH: Michael.

ANDY: And?

JUDITH: I can smell fresh sweat.

ANDY: Yes.

JUDITH: His shirt open, his mouth open on mine. I taste salt from the peanuts he's been eating mixing with salt from his sweat and whenever I smell that from a man in the tube, in the subway, I get turned on.

ANDY: More.

JUDITH: That's it.

ANDY: You have to tell me more.

JUDITH: I have to nothing.

ANDY: Please baby.

JUDITH: Baby!

ANDY: I want to hear about you.

JUDITH: Baby?

ANDY: Why are you so mean?

JUDITH: You're right. I'm a bitch.

ANDY: Tell me something.

JUDITH: What?

ANDY: Anything. I want to hear something. From your life.

JUDITH: OK baby! *(Beat.)* I'm at the top of a lighthouse.[1]

It's summer but the sky's half grey and half black. All around me. Shafts of glare.

ANDY: What happens?

JUDITH: Three hundred and sixty-five stairs. They get narrower. I climb past people going down so that my foot is on this wafer stone. At the top, the wind is so high.

ANDY: I like it!

---

1   This is a reference to the lighthouse at Barfleur, Normandy, France.

JUDITH: There I am standing on this tiny platform. I look over. Nobody. Sand. Pools of water. Sun slashes.

ANDY: How's the sky?

JUDITH: Slate.

ANDY: And the sand.

JUDITH: Moving. I think it's going to break and dead bodies 'll push up, like the End of the World.

ANDY: The End of the World!

JUDITH: And inside me. This huge wave. Screaming. Climb over the rail! Do it!

ANDY: More!

JUDITH: No.

ANDY: *(Violent.)* I said more!

JUDITH: Are you threatening me?

ANDY: Me? I could get wild about you. What do you like?

JUDITH: No!

ANDY: What arouses you?

JUDITH: Bite the side of my hand.

ANDY: Like this? *(She moves in pleasure.)*

JUDITH: And the other. *(He bites the left hand.)*

ANDY: You got what you want now it's my turn.

JUDITH: You want head?

ANDY: Yes. *(Beat.)* Yours. Take me somewhere I've never been.

JUDITH: You're crazy!

ANDY: England. No, France.

JUDITH: France? *(Silence.)*

ANDY: Is that a problem?

JUDITH: None at all.

ANDY: Not Paris. That's such a cliché.

JUDITH: OK.

ANDY: Where are you?

JUDITH: Omaha Beach. The American cemetery. Normandy.

ANDY: You were there with a man? *(Pause.)*

JUDITH: Yes.

ANDY: Michael?

JUDITH: Michael! No!

ANDY: Your husband?

JUDITH: *(Beat.)* Just a man. *(Beat.)* Oh you're sulking! How sweet!

ANDY: You're laughing at me.

JUDITH: Not at all. You're delicious.

ANDY: Omaha. O-m-a-ha![2] Go on.

JUDITH: The sun is hot

ANDY: What's happening?

JUDITH: I am in the GI graveyard. French guards are trying to close the place. It's nearly six.

ANDY: Are they walking with dogs?

JUDITH: No dogs.

ANDY: How are they moving?

JUDITH: In silent cars. Not to disturb the dead.

ANDY: *(Beat.)* Cars or small trucks?

JUDITH: A sort of mini jeep.

ANDY: What do you see?

JUDITH: The grass neat like it's shaved.

ANDY: What else?

JUDITH: Tourists with back packs. Old US military with their middle-aged children.

2   Oma in German means grandmother. Andy is playfully distorting words. He is coincidentally connecting to a key memory in Judith.

ANDY: More. Go on.

JUDITH: I can't. *(ANDY bites her hand again.)*

ANDY: I have to know.

JUDITH: Young men, your age. Boys' graves. Tightly-packed in neat rows stretching as far as the sea. And all those American lads. Running into tank fire. Oh Jesus, I'm a boy soldier pissing my pants!

ANDY: I need to see that place.

JUDITH: Enough!

ANDY: I need this.

JUDITH: Row after row after row 'til your eye hits the water.

ANDY: What?

JUDITH: Simple white crosses and white stars/

ANDY: /Stars?/

JUDITH: /of David. With only the name and the date of death. A name and a date.

ANDY: What do you see?

JUDITH: Tight skin. Sharp jaws. White perfect teeth. Eyes staring in terror. And the guys in the jeeps are screaming in French, get out we're closing, and then the clock strikes six but it doesn't chime like normal French church bells it chimes in French. *(She tries to sing The Star Spangled Banner.)*

ANDY: Angela? *(She doesn't react.)*

ANDY: Tell me your real name.

JUDITH: I can't.

ANDY: Tell me! *(He searches her bag. He finds her passport.)*
Judith.

(She turns towards him and kisses him passionately. He responds.)

(Street sounds of traffic and sirens intensify.)

SCENE FIVE

AN APARTMENT IN MANHATTAN.

West 54th Street.

ANNA: You come round here asking questions. My children never come and here I am in a stinking apartment that the landlord won't fix. No letters, no calls, no emails. Years you don't come. Why now?

JUDITH: It's your birthday.

ANNA: And?

JUDITH: I'm doing a radio story in New York.

ANNA: What about?

JUDITH: A recce. I tell my editor I've got to see Manhattan before I die. I've done New Orleans – Katrina, Los Angeles – Watts, but never here! What took me so long? And I tell Diane, she's my boss but kind of a friend too, I tell her I'll sniff around. Find a few stories. She says OK. And I think, why not come and see you. Hell you're my grandmother's sister. My last living relative. How many years? I was a kid.

ANNA: You running from something?

JUDITH: What?

ANNA: Why you want to see a hundred-ten-year-old woman?

JUDITH: Didn't you want me to come?

ANNA: Look! *(Takes some skin from her arm.)* Hanging off me like a schmatter. Stunner. That was Anna Weib. And I didn't know it. What would I have done if I'd known?

JUDITH: *(Offering her a box with a cake in it.)* Shall we open this?

ANNA: This stinking heat. Every night, smoke in my mouth. The guy next door puffing out the window. Straight to my lungs. Probably the landlord pays him to give me a good cancer. Asshole wants me out.

JUDITH: Who?

ANNA: Damned Jew landlord.

JUDITH: Aren't you protected?

216

ANNA: Yeh but he didn't think I'd live so long. Stinking Yid.
    (Beat.)

Maybe his foreskin grew back.

JUDITH: Is he hassling you?

ANNA: Sticks his son in the upstairs apartment to keep an eye
    on me. And the bastard won't fix the place. You going
    to open that? I didn't eat for four weeks. What am I? A
    ragdoll. Look at this photo of me. If I'd realized how good
    I looked I'd'a had a lot of guys. Look at you. Like drek.
    Why you wear so many clothes? Like a refugee. What's
    wrong with you?

JUDITH: You said you wanted/

ANNA: /You look like shit/

JUDITH: /lots of guys?

ANNA: One to massage my feet, another to rub my legs and
    thighs, and another two to pummel the pain in my ass I got
    with that shyster always trying to get me outta here. And
    for my tits, a couple to sweeten them so they get sassy, pop
    up like when I was young and didn't know how good they
    are.

JUDITH: My husband's having an affair.

ANNA: *(Ignoring this.)* Your parents. Still around?

JUDITH: Both dead.

ANNA: When?

JUDITH: Couple of years ago .

ANNA: Your parents! Who were they? Nobody from nowhere!

JUDITH: Nobody came to their funerals. *(Beat.)*

    Where are your children? *(ANNA ignores this.)* Is there a
    knife here?

ANNA: I'll see him out that lobos. *(Looking up at the ceiling)*
    Look at that damp. And the shower curtain stinks of urine
    but it's not piss. It's mould. *(Beat.)* What husband?

JUDITH: Some older man I married fifteen years back.

ANNA: How old?

JUDITH: Seventy-two. But he's fit and slim.

ANNA: Seventy-two, huh. I could use a toy boy. Can he still shut up?

JUDITH: Not like he used to.

ANNA: Pity. *(Beat.)* This she. His age?

JUDITH: Mine.

ANNA: He takes that stuff to bone up?

JUDITH: Yeh. It's like being battered to death by a rhino

ANNA: So get yourself a young stud. Whaddya need him for?

JUDITH: *(Rips open the cake box.)* I've got it!

ANNA: Give me.

JUDITH: I mean, I've got what to do.

ANNA: Is this chocolate? It's got magnesium. For long life, you know that?

JUDITH: I'll stay with you.

ANNA: What?

JUDITH: This place is huge.

ANNA: Look at that wallpaper. I bought it…. When? When was Suez? Come on.

JUDITH: Suez?

ANNA: Hungary? Got it! Fifty six. Last year a magazine crew shot some photos here. Don't tell him. He'll want a cut.

JUDITH: I'll bring my things over.

ANNA: You see that table. Mahogany. Five bucks from Canal Street. Worth five hundred now

JUDITH: I'm in this crap hotel.

ANNA: And that vase. Louis Quatorze. It's from Paris, France.

JUDITH: Did you go to France?

ANNA: What?

JUDITH: I went there last summer. With my husband. *(Beat.)* Where were you on D-Day?

ANNA: England. The place was full of heavy vehicles and jeeps driving to the coast. Roads so full, whole country was shaking. Why you talking about D-Day? You weren't even born. Where were you? Nowhere. Nobody.

JUDITH: Nobody knows I'm here except my boss.

ANNA: The boss. Louis Quatorze! Isn't that the guy who built Versailles? He had a wife and Madame Pompadour. And lots of mistresses. You never hear of a queen with lots of guys. *(Laughs.)* Well except in Manhattan. *(Eating)* Not bad.

JUDITH: I'll come over in the morning. Move in.

ANNA: What?

JUDITH: With you. *(Beat.)* Is nine OK?

ANNA: *(Eating cake.)* Too much sugar.

JUDITH: I'll do your shopping.

ANNA: I get it sent up.

JUDITH: I'll cook.

ANNA: Nobody cooks!

JUDITH: It'd suit us both.

ANNA: Your meschugenah grandmother. How many times did I ask her to come.

JUDITH: I didn't know that.

ANNA: But no. She wanted to be in England. Didn't want to move again. And what happens? Kaput!

JUDITH: What kaput?

ANNA: Is that dumb or is that dumb?

JUDITH: I'm a great tenant. Hell, I'm family!

ANNA: That's how smart she was.

JUDITH: Who else do you have? I'll talk to the landlord/

ANNA: /Kaput. Putka.[3] Why did she do that?/

JUDITH: /get him to lay off

ANNA: Everything to live for, what was wrong with her?

JUDITH: You have rights.

ANNA: How old was she?

JUDITH: Who?

ANNA: Hungary? Suez? Come on.

JUDITH: Fifty-six.

ANNA: Right. *(Beat.)* A young woman.

JUDITH: I'm fifty-six tomorrow.

ANNA: A child.

JUDITH: I'm moving in Anna.

ANNA: No!

JUDITH: Come on!

ANNA: I don't want you here. You hear me? I don't want nobody.

JUDITH: *(She slaps her own face. ANNA doesn't notice.)* I understand.

ANNA: *(Mocking her English accent)* 'I understand. I understand'.

JUDITH: Forget I asked.

ANNA: I asked her. Yes I did. 'Live with me. We'll figure it out together'. Oh no. Wanted to stay in England. That's what she said. Here were too many people. Here was too much noise. Is that a reason? My kid sister, never had nothing to say. You know you can be too quiet and nobody gives a shit. What did she say when they made her a match with a man she didn't want. Stumm. One man her whole life. One schlang! And then he dies. And what's she got? No husband. No kids nearby. Come here I say and is she even listening? So she's lonely. Is that a reason to do it?

---

3   Kaput means useless or finished. Putka is Anna's use of reversal and word-play to hide grief.

JUDITH: What?

ANNA: Why did she do it?

JUDITH: What? Do what?

ANNA: You don't know?

JUDITH: What?

ANNA: Almost sixty, she didn't have a line on her face, you know that?

JUDITH: What are you telling me?

ANNA: *(Sings.)* Esther Esther sat on a wall

Esther Esther had a great fall

All the kings' horses and all the king's men

JUDITH: Did she have an accident? *(Silence.)*

JUDITH: Tell me. Please!

ANNA: 'Please'! You so damned English

JUDITH: Why was there always silence? Tell me.

ANNA: I'm tired. You should go now.

JUDITH: I've come a long way/

ANNA: /Not as far as I have

JUDITH: Sorry.

ANNA: Sorry? Sorry's not your job. You know how terrible it is when you can't die? Maybe she was lucky. Down into the cool water. No gas. No hanging. No bullet to the brain. No skin drooping like a schmatter.

(JUDITH looks at her.)

The guy. He came to fix some windows. You think he'd be more careful. Sorry. You're not to be sorry. He. He should be sorry. What do I do? Sue him for malfeasance? Look at me. Bruised all over. Last week, he leaves his toolbox and down I go. Flat. On. My. Back. Missionary position but there ain't no preacher on top of me. *(Laughs.)* If you're shtupping and you get on top he sees your face hang. All my friends, broken hips, broken femurs, everything they got made new again. Me? I can't break. Why you come here? Recce? You even speak English?

JUDITH: Reconnoitre. First meaning, check out a place for future war. Second meaning. Check out future radio programme. Brooklyn Bridge. My job, check it out. It's an amazing icon. Most Brits hardly know it.

ANNA: Everyone's snooping around. And now you. You always were a nosey bitch.

JUDITH: Nosey is how I make my living.

ANNA: This husband of yours? He left you?

JUDITH: He wants me back. He won't get rid of her but he wants me back

ANNA: How many husbands did I have?

JUDITH: Three.

ANNA: Only three?

JUDITH: Did she really kill herself? *(Silence.)*

ANNA: When we were kids we had cats and they made her drown the kittens. She always howled and still they made her do it. Then she did it to herself. *(Beat.)* And you! If I had a body like yours what wouldn't I do. *(Pause.)*

But you dress like a shlumper. You got to smarten up lady. Look at me. Do I let myself go? Do I? When I was in Manchester with her I bought her this fancy coat in Kendals.⁴ The fog it was so yellow you couldn't see your hand in front. The coat. Cut loose. A-Line. Powder blue. Real angora. Cost me a week's wages. And she! She put weights in the pockets. Flat irons. She couldn't even swim, the stupid bitch. *(Looks up and shouts.)* You bastard! I won't leave this stinking planet for as long as you live. *(Laughs.)* Look at me, you asshole! I've got family! What've you got? A drek son, lungs full of tar, belly full of schmaltz. Look at me, I'm telling you, look at me! Here I am paying peanuts in a great apartment eating high class chocolate gateau with

---

4   Kendal, Milne & Co in Manchester, England. At the time of reference it was a fancy department store.

my relative from London-England. And here I am! Five minutes from Times Square! Eight minutes from Carnegie Hall! Ten minutes from Columbus Circle! All that hiked-up rent you're missing well you can whistle Dixie because I've twenty more years left in me. You know what schmuck, I'll be dancing on your grave long after you're farted out of a worm's ass.

SCENE SIX

THE NEW YORK SUBWAY.

This is the journey downtown to City Hall.

(JUDITH is standing on the platform edge. She is carrying a small tape recorder.)

(Sound of the oncoming train. It gets louder and louder.)

JUDITH: It's the Six. Red lights. Like a dressing room mirror.

(Train pulls in. Doors open.)

MALE V/O: Please stand clear of the closing doors.

WOMAN Y: Excuse me. Is this train going downtown?

JUDITH: Uptown or downtown or in my lady's chamber?

(Two notes <bing bong> to announce voice-over to passengers.)

MALE V/O: Please stand clear of the closing doors.

(JUDITH gets on the subway.)

(Voice mix of a group of people standing up talking.)

WOMAN K: And what? Madison and what?

MAN R: You remember that time? You and me?

(Woman laughs.)

V/O: Please stand clear of the closing doors.

WOMAN K: Lady, I tell her, it runs between a hundred and thirty-eight and twenty-third. *(Loud and irritable.)* What's the cross street?

MAN G: I just wanted to live a few hours with her. Two, three times a week. What's wrong with that?

OK I kissed her. But that's all. Well that's what I told her. 'I kissed her, I kissed her, I kissed! OK?'

WOMAN V/O: The next stop is Fourteenth Street

MAN G: And so I say OK and we go and you know what?

WOMAN B: I was leaving the office late. He was my boss.

MAN G: He's my shrink, not hers, and you know what he says?

WOMAN Y: *(Shouting.)* Is this a local or an express?

WOMAN B: And he took me in his arms.

MAN G: The shrink, could be my son, he says, 'you come to see me together' and we go and you know what? He says, 'You don't listen to your wife'. Can you believe that? You don't listen to your wife!

WOMAN B *(80)*: I left my husband and my two young sons for him.

MAN G: She never stops yakking.

WOMAN B *(80)*: And him, he didn't even want to divorce his wife.

WOMAN H: I was driving and I see this sign on the gas station.

'My boss is a Jewish carpenter'! Takes me a while to get it

WOMAN B: And I knew I'd done wrong. The boys. I kept seeing their faces. And I asked my husband, I want to come back...

MAN G: And he asks me, this guy, he asks me, 'but what do you feel now?' and he's thumping his gut, 'in here? What do you feel godamnit.'

WOMAN B: ...but he said no.

MAN G: He tells me 'Be a man'. This kid old enough to be my son!

WOMAN B: So I never did go back to the boys. They're men now. My sons. Retirees! Imagine!

MAN C (70S): And you know? She brings me over her real interesting friends and she leaves me alone with them.

WOMAN ANNOUNCER: Chambers Street. This is Chambers Street.

WOMAN H: I got it! Jesus. That's not his real name!

MAN C: This goddess. Six foot blonde with a square jaw and a look cuts right through your vital arteries. Tells me her name is Missy.

BUSKER: Ladies and gentlemen. I'm not going to tell you that my cat died.

WOMAN B: I left two boys for a miser. My son he's sixty years old. And can you believe this. He still blames me for leaving.

MAN C: 'Missy'. What kind of a name is that for a grown woman?

WOMAN B: He still cries!

BUSKER: ...or that my dog got eaten alive by fleas. I'm not going to tell you that I'm hungry and homeless. I'm going to tell you what I do. I am a poet. And I'm going to offer you one of my own poems.

MALE V/O: Next stop is Brooklyn Bridge. City Hall.

BUSKER: So whatever you can spare from your hearts. God bless you. But first of all I'll tell you my name. It's 'Forever'.

MAN Z *(Older Black guy)*: Hey lady you got kids?

JUDITH: No.

MAN Z: You spend a night with me, I'll give you kids.

(JUDITH laughs.)

SCENE SEVEN

BROOKLYN BRIDGE

(Sound of cars and horns. Sounds of people walking across the bridge.)

JUDITH: *(Into her tape recorder)* Testing. Diane. OK this is Judith. Doing the recce. Talking to my editor. Doing all the right things.

(She changes into conversational mode.)

Hey! Wish I were in De Martino's[5] with you drinking Chianti and you telling me about some important producers' meeting and you getting flashes of your new guy doing it to you!

(Back to professional.) So I'm coming out of the subway. I'm looking up and inside my head The Flat Iron Building. And The Chrysler. And the Empire State.

(To herself.) And inside it's Ground Zero. *(She smacks her face.)*

(Light change.)

(Back to professional.) Out at City Hall, I'm turning left and walking past the traffic. The road curves. And there it is!

(At the beginning of The Bridge from the Manhattan end. A man is hanging off a cable one arm outstretched posing for the camera. A woman with an "I Heart New York" T shirt is posing Monroe-style for the camera. Other cast members are walking towards the Bridge taking photos. Reverse so that the audience becomes The Bridge.)

(Exhalation of breath.)

Oh God. So long. So wide. So high!

(Sound of cars going by. A hospital worker in blue scrubs eats a bagel and is listening to the radio on headphones.)

Radio

MALE V/O: Another fine day across the city, high around 70 but a chance of showers 74 degrees in Central Park… weather station, Ted Dibley….

(Sound of helicopter. Sound of car horns. Sound of traffic intensifies.)

VOICE OFF: Open your heart to divine love! Come and shake your soul!

(During this speech a man passes on rollerblades. A woman jogs. JUDITH dodges them.)

---

5   Da Martino's is an Italian restaurant in Great Portland Street, London. It is not far from the BBC radio centre in Portland Place.

JUDITH: *(Back to tape recorder.)* OK Diane. I am trying to follow your example. I wake up this morning and there's this Adonis next to me. Young guys. I'd forgotten they can do it over and over.

VOICE OFF: Open your heart to divine love!

JUDITH: And the first time is just the getting ready and the second is good but the third/

VOICE OFF: /Come and shake your soul!/

JUDITH: /is really head breaking!

VOICE OFF: Jesus Christ, he loves you!

JUDITH: You think we can do a feature on that? What shall we call it? The third coming! *(She giggles.)*

(Sound of Chinese music on someone's radio as they jog past.)

OK, suppose we go for the Brooklyn Bridge anniversary idea. Question is which? What's the hook? First day of construction? First jumper? First plot to destroy? *(She inhales.)*

Hell Diane, the span of it all, walking from Manhattan to Brooklyn. Wow the drop into the East River!

VOICE OFF: He died that you may live!

JUDITH: Just listen. *(Holding up her mike to the sky. Sound of helicopters intensifies.)*

VOICE OFF: Just get the Jewish people back to I-s-r-e-a-l and the Lord is coming!

(GLORIA passes by wearing NYPD uniform.)

JUDITH: Hey officer.

GLORIA: Can I help you ma'am?

JUDITH: This your beat?

GLORIA: Maybe.

JUDITH: *(Showing her press card.)* Can I talk to you?

GLORIA: You need to speak to our press office.

JUDITH: Just a few words.

GLORIA: I'm busy lady.

JUDITH: It won't take long.

GLORIA: I'm expected/

JUDITH: /Two minutes/

GLORIA: /at the precinct

JUDITH: You see people jump from here?

GLORIA: What?

JUDITH: Suicides?

GLORIA: Why you asking?

JUDITH: It's an idea for a story.

GLORIA: You from *The London Times*?

JUDITH: BBC Radio.

GLORIA: Radio huh. You talk funny. Like the queen!

JUDITH: Not quite. *(Beat.)* Tell me something. You get a lot of suicides here?

GLORIA: A few. But mostly they go to The Golden Gate. Here you need to walk the high wire.

JUDITH: *(Looking at the suspension wiring.)* I was expecting....

GLORIA: Last Wednesday there was a floater....

JUDITH: ...what? Something like Waterloo Bridge...

GLORIA: Fourteen year old Chinese American flunked his exams....

JUDITH: ...not two motorways.

GLORIA: ...couldn't face telling his parents.

JUDITH: All the photos and the films of here. You only see this part. Never those roads down there. I mean if you jumped splat under a Chrysler.

GLORIA: What?

JUDITH: *(Recording.)* So it's mainly kids?

GLORIA: *(Beat.)* All kinds. Something about this view makes them crazy. No they're crazy first. *(She is wary.)*

You really should talk to our press office.

JUDITH: The problem is I don't want the official line. I need the personal.

GLORIA: Yeh, well I don't know. NYPD. Everyone wants a piece. Movies, novelists. We get strict instructions. *(Looking at her phone.)* I'm sure I have a number for public relations.

JUDITH: I understand but these things take weeks. But please Officer, I've an early morning flight. I need something now.

GLORIA: I don't know.

JUDITH: That kid that jumped, the Chinese American?

GLORIA: That's more of an impulse thing. A serious jumper checks into a high-rise hotel. Opens a window.

JUDITH: There are two types?

GLORIA: Sorry lady. I'm not allowed. If you want information you really need to talk to ESU. Emergency Service Unit. It's their specialty. I'm homicide. Look I really have to go.

JUDITH: One more minute?

GLORIA: I've got to get to my retirement party.

JUDITH: What?

GLORIA: Starts in half an hour

JUDITH: How old are you?

GLORIA: We can get our pension at forty four.

JUDITH: You look thirty!

GLORIA: I have two daughters. They ask me 'when you going to come home in a box mommy?'

JUDITH: Oh.

GLORIA: So you see, it's not just about age.

JUDITH: You must be crazy about them.

GLORIA: Sure I am.

JUDITH: How old are they?

GLORIA: Eight and ten.

JUDITH: What are their names?

GLORIA: *(Beat.)* You got kids?

JUDITH: No.

GLORIA: So nobody needs you to be home.

JUDITH: Right.

GLORIA: Sorry I didn't mean it that way. *(Beat.)* Today's a big day for me. Got to go lady.

JUDITH: Glad I am part of your big day then.

GLORIA: Problem is....

JUDITH: Yes?

GLORIA: I'm crazy about my job.

JUDITH: And crazy about your kids.

GLORIA: And I can't have both.

JUDITH: Why not?

GLORIA: Every morning. I wake up frozen. I see my girls, watching me in a coffin.

JUDITH: Shit.

GLORIA: I want to sleep a whole night/

JUDITH: /Won't you miss/

GLORIA: /is that too much to ask?

JUDITH: /all this?

GLORIA: I'll take a break and then I'll go private.

JUDITH: That's good?

GLORIA: It's safer.

JUDITH: Private detective. Doing what? Spying on cheating husbands?

GLORIA: What a drag.

JUDITH: Won't you miss your buddies?

GLORIA: Sure. They're kind of family.

JUDITH: And the adrenaline kick? How will you get that?

GLORIA: You weird.

JUDITH: Why do you say that?

GLORIA: Lady from nowhere. Suddenly you're inside my brain. You shoulda been a cop.

JUDITH: I'm a coward.

GLORIA: We all are.

JUDITH: Not you. *(Beat.)* You got a husband?

GLORIA: Why you ask?

JUDITH: I don't know.

GLORIA: Ryan's waiting for me at the precinct.

JUDITH: He's a cop?

GLORIA: Yeh.

JUDITH: And he wants you to retire?

GLORIA: How do you know that?

JUDITH: That way you're home with the girls.

GLORIA: He says it's the right decision.

JUDITH: And you?

GLORIA: *(Beat.)* Hell! In thirty minutes I'll be drinking champagne and all the boys will be there. Tonight I'll sleep calm.

JUDITH: You'll miss the streets.

GLORIA: I'll get over it.

JUDITH: And if you don't?

GLORIA: New life. My own boss.

JUDITH: Taxes, invoices.

GLORIA: My mom was home for me. I gotta do the same for my girls. Your mom work?

JUDITH: You mind if I switch this on?

GLORIA: My last day. What the hell.

(JUDITH turns on the tape.)

JUDITH: So Officer *(Looking at her tag.)* Ryan? Ryan-Sanchez?

GLORIA: Irish husband. Parents from Puerto Rico. Look how they label us. Like a grocery store. Very low class. *(She takes out paper but doesn't read it.)* I gotta give this speech.

JUDITH: Can I hear?

GLORIA: Bad luck. *(She puts it back in her pocket.)* Like the groom seeing the bride's dress. Today my job is bring that Gloria Sanchez Virgin Cop into the party with me. Can you believe, twenty one year old rookie in South Jamaica.

JUDITH: Where's that?

GLORIA: Way out in Queens.

JUDITH: Was the rookie scared?

GLORIA: Excited to death. We go in and there he is. My first cadaver. Spider crawling out of his nose. And the phone goes in his apartment. Some guy. 'Is Jerry there?' I tell him 'Jerry can't talk to you right now'. And he says 'why not?' 'Cos he's a dead man.' And he's screaming 'Oh my God, he's dead! Oh my God, he's dead!' And you're not supposed to do that, it has to be face to face but how can it be face to face when the guy's on the phone. You really recording this?

JUDITH: You mind?

GLORIA: You putting me on radio?

JUDITH: No.

GLORIA: You could get me fired

JUDITH: Aren't you retiring?

GLORIA: *(She shrugs.)* You gotta cigarette? *(Rubs her neck.)*

JUDITH: I don't smoke. Are you in pain?

GLORIA: I have these cadaver bones in my neck. He musta been a smoker and I'm dreaming cigarettes.

JUDITH: How did you get them?

GLORIA: I'm out on a chase. I fall out of a police car straight on to my neck. They give me new bits. The question is whose body is in me?

JUDITH: That's scary.

GLORIA: I'm getting too old to be spinning around pavements on my spine.

Ryan's right. I should get out of this. Look at me. All held together with steel pins and metal plates.

JUDITH: You look like Hollywood.

GLORIA: Yeh but inside I'm all through.

JUDITH: Are you? *(Beat.)*

Why did you go for homicide? Isn't that the boys' territory?

GLORIA: Because I'm no girl desk cop. All that worrying about can I get home for five and make dinner crap. You want some bagel. *(Has two and offers one.)* Only go to waste.

JUDITH: I don't eat wheat.

GLORIA: You one these health freaks? You look like a stick insect. I know. No carbs. *(She eats.)* OK, so pick out the lox and throw the rest. *(JUDITH looks at the bagel and eats. Silence while they both chew.)* You think there's too much cream cheese? *(Pause.)* You know, if I was a guy I'd live off selling spunk.

JUDITH: What?

GLORIA: Hundreds of gallons, every day, thrown in the trash. I get to thinking that, in that mess, is my child. He may be Black, Chinese, Caucasian or Indian. Now, he looks like snot. Sorry I'm putting you off.

JUDITH: I like the way you talk.

GLORIA: I like the way you listen.

JUDITH: When did you want to be a cop?

GLORIA: Maybe seven. *(Beat.)*

JUDITH: Tell me.

GLORIA: I'm out in the street. Guy falls out of a window. White gunge coming out of his ears. Then the cops come and I want to be running hard with those guys.

JUDITH: Amazing!

GLORIA: Now why would a grown man jump?

JUDITH: Your parents want you to join the police?

GLORIA: Sure. I was brought up strict Puerto Rican. Even in the projects. Other girls out late with boys. Not me. My mom. You study. You stay home. You have a mom like that?

JUDITH: No.

GLORIA: How was yours?

JUDITH: My 'mom'. She wasn't around much.

GLORIA: Who looked after you?

JUDITH: Some old woman. *(Beat.)* Nobody.

(Judith moves off the walkway and climbs up to the side bridge. SUSAN enters looking disheveled. Nobody notices her.)

GLORIA: Nobody. This old woman must've been somebody.

SUSAN: Hey officer?

GLORIA: Yes Miss?

SUSAN: I've asked about a hundred people already in this city.

I was in the 17th Street precinct. I walked all the way from there. I need some cash. The cops there, they wouldn't listen

GLORIA: Beat it.

SUSAN: I had a fight with my boyfriend. Kicked me in the head, you hear me? I left the apartment and I came to the cops and I walked out with no cash, you hear me?

GLORIA: Move it. Now!

SUSAN: I've not eaten for days. I went to the store. For fish. Black kid behind the counter. I tell him what you throw away, could you see yourself just putting it in a bag for me? Only goes in the garbage. And he says, 'I can't give you no fish but I can give you something'. *(JUDITH records SUSAN.)*

And I'm thinking he'll give me some roe or maybe a can of tuna and he says, 'Lady, all I can give you right now is my name'. Then he holds out his hands like this. 'Gabriel'. Like he was some fucking angel. You see if you could just let me have a few dollars. You, what you doing? You recording?

JUDITH: Free country.

SUSAN: You got my voice in your machine?

GLORIA: Get outta here.

SUSAN: What if I jump off of here, you could sell it. You take a photo?

JUDITH: *(Beat.)* If someone were to jump, I mean if I were to jump, wouldn't this be the perfect spot? A woman, my size. All she needs to do is climb over.

SUSAN: She's stealing my soul, officer.

JUDITH: *(As she moves out. Talks to herself.)* Get to the arc lights and keep going.

SUSAN: What about you Miss? You gotta few dollars in your purse?

GLORIA: Hey English! What the hell you doing?

(JUDITH pulls a cocktail dress out of her bag and changes into it.)

This some kind of game?

JUDITH: It's my birthday. Hungary. Suez. Fifty six. Get it? I'm giving my husband a present. *(She photographs herself with her phone.)*

GLORIA: I don't see no husband.

JUDITH: Me neither!

GLORIA: Get down! Now! Everyone's gonna call 911. You'll be surrounded.

(Takes out phone.)

SUSAN: Maybe a five dollar bill?

JUDITH: It's OK. *(She turns off her machine.)*

GLORIA: What?

JUDITH: It's an experiment. To see how it feels. Relax.

GLORIA: Stop fooling around. Get down!

JUDITH: *(She is quite far out on the girder.)* Now I can breathe! First time in weeks.

GLORIA: English, that's enough!

JUDITH: NO! Go to your party.

GLORIA: I'm going nowhere.

JUDITH: Oh God I had no idea it would feel like this!

You ever been out here? Maybe that cadaver you got jumped and hit the road.

GLORIA: I got you wrong. I'm losing it. I thought you were like me.

JUDITH: Like you?

SUSAN: Lady, look in your pocket? Your purse? Maybe a spare dollar?

GLORIA: You got family?

JUDITH: What?

GLORIA: Someone I can call? What's your name?

JUDITH: You saw my press card.

GLORIA: I didn't catch/

JUDITH: /Forget it/

GLORIA: /your name? *(Beat.)* Why you doing this?

JUDITH: It's incredible. Like a stone gone from my chest!

GLORIA: You making me late.

JUDITH: So go!

GLORIA: I gotta be at the precinct in fifteen. *(She's talking fast as she thinks what to do.)* You thinking about jumping? It's a filthy way to die.

SUSAN: Who's talking about dying? *(She sits and watches.)*

V/O: Hey! Sanchez. What's up?

GLORIA: *(To offstage, cops coming towards her.)* Cool it guys!

JUDITH: You let them near here and I swear to God.

GLORIA: *(Yelling at the cops.)* Keep your distance.

JUDITH: You tell them!

GLORIA: Rivera's making a cordon. Nobody can cross the Bridge. You gonna stop the whole of New York City. You want to paralyze Manhattan to Brooklyn.

JUDITH: Manhattan to Brooklyn! How about that!

GLORIA: Why you doing this?

JUDITH: Humpty Dumpty sat on a wall.

GLORIA: What?

JUDITH: Your grandmother still alive?

GLORIA: What?

JUDITH: Is she?

GLORIA: What's with the grandmother?

JUDITH: Forget it.

GLORIA: Who is she? Your mother's mother?

JUDITH: Sometimes I hear her voice.

GLORIA: Tell me about her. *(Silence.)*

JUDITH: Had a great fall. You learn that in America? *(Beat.)* Oh God! Look at her. That's the Statue of Liberty?!! She's amazing! Did you know France gave it to America? And America gave France her boys.

GLORIA: You ready to come down now?

JUDITH: *(Looking out across the River to the Statue of Liberty.)* It's like the End of the World. There's nothing but me, the city and this water. All I need is enough courage to jump and then. Nothing.

GLORIA: Not true! You'll be in agony even before you hit water. One massive, bursting heart. You really want that?

(Struggling to win her attention, she fixes on JUDITH's shoes.)

What are they? The- latest-Paris-fashion-walking-off-the-bridge shoes?

JUDITH: A suicide takes them off, then she jumps.

GLORIA: Where you hear that crap? And this is about what? Some guy? You screw my important day. For some creep?

JUDITH: Turn around. Walk away.

GLORIA: I can't.

MAN/OFF: Hey you up there! Make my day! Jump!

JUDITH: When I'm ready not when you tell me you piece of shit.

GLORIA: Move that vehicle you asshole before I have you arrested.

MAN/off: It's a free country officer!

GLORIA: Move it fast or I'll have you banged up for incitement to murder. Now English. I'm running out of time here.

(She waves the paper with her speech on it.)

JUDITH: Walk lady. Go. Read your speech. Have a great life! *(Silence.)*

GLORIA: OK. Here's the deal.

JUDITH: What?

GLORIA: I give you my speech, you give me a step.

JUDITH: Fuck your speech.

GLORIA: You don't mean that.

JUDITH: Don't I?

GLORIA: You and me. We the same. We need to know. It's what keeps us alive isn't it. Find out stuff?

(They stare at each other.)

You in deep trouble lady. Want me to call for help?

JUDITH: Want me to go over? *(Silence.)*

GLORIA: OK. OK. Listen, I'm going to make you an offer.

JUDITH: Not interested. Hey cop. You never saw me.

GLORIA: I can't do that.

JUDITH: Why not?

GLORIA: I serve the city.

JUDITH: You're retired.

GLORIA: Not yet.

JUDITH: They're waiting for you.

GLORIA: Here's the story.

JUDITH: What?

GLORIA: I give you what you want. You give me something back.

JUDITH: No deal. *(Moves away towards the edge.)* I like being here. You know that!

GLORIA: One fucking inch. *(Silence.)*

GLORIA: You want me to beg? *(GLORIA gets down on her knees.)*

Look at what I'm doing. You see this? Look at me. Kneeling!

This I only do for Jesus and his holy mother. What do you want English? *(Silence.)*

JUDITH: Your first day.

GLORIA: What?

JUDITH: As that virgin cop. Give me Sanchez before she meets Ryan.

GLORIA: First you move and I don't want some friggin' gnat step

(JUDITH takes a small step back towards GLORIA.)

Good. Now turn that thing on.

(JUDITH switches on her recorder.)

JUDITH: I'm waiting.

GLORIA: OK. I'm in an apartment on Lexington Avenue.

JUDITH: And?

GLORIA: Roaches. Millions of them. Big black fuckers. Stinking like a dead person.

JUDITH: Go on.

GLORIA: A young woman's been shot. She's lying on the bed. I'm looking for a piece and I see something black in a drawer and I put my hand inside and it moves! There are millions of the bastards. From the walls, from the carpet, running all over me.

(Enter LOUISE.)

LOUISE: Hey Detective.

GLORIA: *(Mock polite to LOUISE.)* Can I help you?

SUSAN: Nobody helps, nobody here. Go screw yourself.

(To LOUISE.) A few dollars, you got something for me lady?

GLORIA: Look English, I'm holding out for you. Now there's these two crazies. Give me a break. One more step.

LOUISE: Who you talking to?

GLORIA: Look over there grandma.

LOUISE: Oh. Oh! Oh!

JUDITH: Who's grandma?

GLORIA: So you see if it's not urgent.

LOUISE: Last Christmas. I went to visit my daughter. All the way from Queens out to Westchester. It was snowing. To see the baby.

GLORIA: Move it.

LOUISE: And when I get there she says you can't stay. You have to go to a hotel. In their warm house with fancy wooden floors you have to take your shoes off and her dog, all powdered and in a tiny mink coat, he gets better attention than I do. In a hotel she says when their house is full with empty bedrooms.

GLORIA: OK now move on.

LOUISE: And she gives me some food on plastic plates and plastic cutlery. What's the matter? You too fancy to wash dishes?

GLORIA: I'm not telling you again.

LOUISE: In Poland/

JUDITH: /Poland?

LOUISE: / after 1945, if any kids had parents or grandparents, we knew they were Catholic. I even learned their prayers and everyone believed me.

Hail Mary full of Grace the Lord is with thee.

GLORIA: Blessed be the fruit of thy womb. Now grandma Jesus will really love you if you get outta here.

LOUISE: I was thinking officer, if you come with me to their place and tell them, then they'll understand. I'm an American. I have rights. Don't I have rights officer. Rights to see my own grandchildren?

JUDITH: Hello grandma. Where you from?

LOUISE: Where you think? Where they tattoo your arms with kisses?

JUDITH: You were there?

SUSAN: You got some money for me?

LOUISE: *(Looking up)* What's Madame doing up there?

JUDITH: Were you?

SUSAN: You make me sick to my stomach

LOUISE: My daughter. She's working in a beauty parlor.

SUSAN: You hear what I'm saying?

(SUSAN leaves.)

LOUISE: No two the same. Like a fingerprint. That's what she says. Brazilian. What does she know of South America? She's never been out of Queens. *(Looks up.)* Nice shoes.

JUDITH: You want them?

GLORIA: No!

LOUISE: You think if I give them my daughter she'll let me see the kids?

JUDITH: Catch? *(She takes off a shoe and holds it up. LOUISE catches it.)*

GLORIA: Shit.

LOUISE: She's a 9. Big feet for a small girl. Helps you run fast. *(She tries it on.)*

I need the other. Oh look! You've got a fancy machine!

GLORIA: I'm telling you for the last time.

(JUDITH takes off second shoe and carries it in her hand. She switches off her tape.)

LOUISE: She's an English major. Goes up to people. Asks if they know the difference between 'I have no mother did you know that?' and 'I have no mother, comma, did you know that?'

JUDITH: Nobody has a mother these days.

LOUISE: Now I'm no shrink but to me that's aggressive. You think that's aggressive?

(JUDITH's phone rings. She looks at the screen.)

JUDITH: *(She listens.)* Where am I? Where are you? You told her to go to hell yet?

GLORIA: *(Yelling offstage to another cop.)* It's OK Rivera. I'm handling this.

JUDITH: What do I want? I want to feel her twisted mouth under my heel. *(Beat.)* I'm on Brooklyn Bridge! That's where. *(She switches it off.)*

GLORIA: Your husband screwing around?

JUDITH: Leave me alone.

GLORIA: That's why you want to jump? Is that it? Now I am calling for back-up.

JUDITH: You do that and I'm going out there.

GLORIA: *(Deciding to change tactics.)* You think sometimes I don't want to end it all?

JUDITH: You?

GLORIA: 'You are a piece of crap. You always was a piece of crap. You always will be a piece of crap'. That's the voice in my head when I walk in front of traffic late night with the headlamps in my eyes.

JUDITH: You do that? *(Turns on machine in such a way that it's as if she isn't aware of her action.)*

(During the next speech JUDITH comes down from the third arc light to the one nearest GLORIA's. She is listening.)

GLORIA: And the cars stop and the drivers scream at me. So I go home. Everyone's asleep. I take out my gun and I polish the barrel. And I hold it to my head. And you know what stops me pulling that trigger? A photo by my bed. Me and 946 police cadets. Company 57. Graduation Day in Madison Square Garden. And they throw the confetti at us. Like it's a wedding. And I'm getting married to the city. You getting this in that machine?

JUDITH: Yes.

GLORIA: I'm giving my life to protect the 1.75 miles between Canal Street and the lowest tip of Manhattan And in that photo there's me and the Mayor shaking hands. And then again with it. 'You're trash. No matter how many times you shake hands with the Mayor you ain't never going to wash off the smell of your own shit.'

JUDITH: OK.

GLORIA: And the only thing that stops me, it's not my husband, it's not my girls. It's knowing I can put on this uniform day after day and when I wear it then I'm somebody. *(Beat.)* And you know what English, I don't think I can go on not doing that.

(A police car passes and the blue light is flashing.)

JUDITH: Get him away from here!

GLORIA: You really want to jump because of a guy?

JUDITH: What do you know!

GLORIA: There's got to be at least one person who cares for you.

JUDITH: Really?

GLORIA: Your mother? *(JUDITH laughs for a long time.)*

GLORIA: You angry with her? You mad at her and you take it out on your husband.

JUDITH: *(Beat.)* What's this? Some cop shrink bullshit? Go to hell.

(Turns off her machine.) When I've gone at least he'll know who I am.

GLORIA: What you doing. Never works. *(Silence.)*

GLORIA: You listening English?

JUDITH: What?

GLORIA: You want to know about dying? I'll tell you stuff I never told nobody.

JUDITH: What? *(She switches on her tape recorder secretly.)*

GLORIA: You want my first homicide?

JUDITH: I don't care.

GLORIA: So why you switched on?

JUDITH: No reason.

GLORIA: This young woman. Actress. Lived in Soho. In her condo, these construction workers they were bugging her. Noise all day long, she can't sleep. All night she's working tables in a restaurant and all day she needs rest. Goes down to see the guys.

JUDITH: What guys?

GLORIA: Immigrants. No English. First she's polite but soon she's telling them 'fuck off' on a regular basis.

JUDITH: Come on!

GLORIA: One night she comes back home and there's one guy and it's four in the morning and he's still making noise so she yells at him and he hits her and she falls down. So he gets scared. Takes her upstairs to her apartment. Into the shower. She's out cold but she's not dead. So he takes her belt and he strangles her. But he makes it look like suicide. And for the next few days all her friends are leaving messages but she never answers. Someone calls 911.

JUDITH: You get the call?

JUDITH: We go in there. And the friends say no way it's suicide. She has a husband. She has a young kid. She has auditions. *(Her phone rings.)*

JUDITH: Don't take it!

GLORIA: I gotta.

JUDITH: I said no.

GLORIA: It's the precinct. They're waiting for me.

JUDITH: That girl?

GLORIA: Yeh.

JUDITH: What happened? *(Phone stops ringing.)*

(Silence.)

(Yelling.) I said what happened?

GLORIA: Check your machine!

JUDITH: It's on, damn you!

GLORIA: I did the confession.

JUDITH: Just you?

GLORIA: Yeh. He tells me, after he knocks her down and sees she's hurt. He's frightened she'll go to the cops. Terrified he'll get deported.

JUDITH: The woman. Who is she?

GLORIA: Russian. Jew. Been here ten years.

JUDITH: Oh?

GLORIA: You a Jew English?

JUDITH: What was her name?

GLORIA: Kozinskaya.

JUDITH: Where from?

GLORIA: Moscow. Came when she was a kid. This we find out from the family. We go to her apartment. We find his footprint on the toilet seat. I tell him I know it's you. And he says no.

JUDITH: In the precinct? Just you and him?

GLORIA: That's right.

JUDITH: What do you feel?

GLORIA: His sweat. Kinda rancid. Gets up my nose. I'm kinda trying not to breathe in. All I know is I've got to get the story.

JUDITH: Go on.

GLORIA: His body is screaming for nicotine and caffeine. No coffee. No cigarettes. So he gets real tired. Me, I'm drinking coffee. And he's all on edge.

JUDITH: What does he say?

GLORIA: Tells me how he hit her and she banged her head on concrete. He feels a pulse and thinks she's dead and she looks so beautiful in his arms and maybe he can fuck her.

JUDITH: Does he do that?

GLORIA: No time. He's got to move fast. So he takes the belt from her jeans and hangs it from the metal rod at the window and he stands on the toilet seat. *(Points to the recorder.)* Check it's working.

JUDITH: OK.

GLORIA: He says she's real heavy for a light woman and all the time he's telling me he's sobbing like a kid.

JUDITH: *(Applauds mockingly.)* You one helluva cop.

GLORIA: Sure. I'm Jesus Christ's right hand. Come on. *(She doesn't move.)* Don't you come from a people they always trying to kill?

JUDITH: Shut up!

(Her phone rings again. She looks at it not sure whether to answer. It rings through the next speeches.)

GLORIA: And you want to end it because your guy puts his dick in some other woman? You kill yourself for that? That's not it. There's got to be something else.

JUDITH: I said shut it.

GLORIA: What's the story?

JUDITH: No story.

GLORIA: I don't believe you.

JUDITH: What do you care?

GLORIA: I don't. But then I'm here. Now. With you English. So something tells me I do care. *(Silence.)*

JUDITH: For what?

GLORIA: You, you bitch!

(Silence.)

I'm waiting. You got something in here *(Thumps heart.)* and I want to know what it is.

JUDITH: Nothing. *(She thumps her chest.)* A stone to help me sink. *(JUDITH seems upset. Silence.)*

GLORIA: What you thinking, English?

JUDITH: Nothing. Nothing. Nothing. You're the one wants to talk.

GLORIA: You owe me/

JUDITH: /nothing!

GLORIA: I got down on my knees and begged. I begged to you. Jesus Christ!

What else do you want from me? *(Pause.)* Jesus, I'm trying to save a life here.

JUDITH: Trying to save the dead.

GLORIA: What dead?

JUDITH: My grandmother.

GLORIA: Yes! That's it!

JUDITH: What?

GLORIA: What did she say to you?

JUDITH: When?

GLORIA: When you were a kid?

JUDITH: Nothing

GLORIA: Stop this!

JUDITH: *(Beat.)* She said I had strong limbs. I didn't know what that word meant. I see her looking at me. Kind of amazed that I am alive. *(Beat.)* She lost a lot of people.

GLORIA: What people? *(Silence.)*

What does that mean, she lost a lot of people?

(Silence.)

GLORIA: You've got to live for her.

JUDITH: I've got to die for her.

GLORIA: You love her.

JUDITH: You can't love the dead Sanchez.

LOUISE: *(Half asleep.)* I went to Church and looked at the lovely lady with the baby.

GLORIA: Can't you?

LOUISE: ...the fruit of thy womb, Jesus!

GLORIA: That's it! It's not the husband. It's her!

LOUISE: He died that you are saved! That's something!

GLORIA: And you think jumping brings you together?

JUDITH: Maybe.

GLORIA: That's bullshit.

JUDITH: Is it?

GLORIA: You're here now with me. Not her. And you and me. We've got a deal.

JUDITH: Did I say yes to your crap deal?

GLORIA: One more step.   *(GLORIA's phone rings.)*

JUDITH: Don't take it!

GLORIA: I gotta.

JUDITH: I said no.

GLORIA: It's Ryan. He's waiting for me.

JUDITH: Leave me alone. I don't want you to see.

GLORIA: You're smart. You're good-looking. You got your whole life.

(JUDITH's phone rings. She looks at it not sure whether to answer. It rings through the next speeches.)

GLORIA: You've got friends.

JUDITH: I've got nothing. What do you know with your good cop shit. Fuck you.

GLORIA: And fuck you. Go on. Jump. Fuck up my day. My party. My whole life. But, if you go, then I'm sure as hell going to watch.

JUDITH: No way!

GLORIA: You fuck my day lady/

JUDITH: /I won't let you.

(Her phone stops ringing. Police cars are coming close. Their blue lights are flashing. Sound of helicopters.)

JUDITH: They've stopped the traffic. Did you do that?

GLORIA: *(Yelling off.)* I'm telling you hold it guys. I've got this controlled.

(JUDITH's phone rings again. The ringing gets louder and louder. She throws the phone at GLORIA who catches it)

JUDITH: Tell him this is what he gets for fucking her.

GLORIA: This isn't about him. Don't do this! God loves you!

JUDITH: God! You and your sentimental Christian shit.

GLORIA: You can't just end it.

JUDITH: Watch me!

GLORIA: Your grandmother. What was her name?

JUDITH: None of your business.

GLORIA: You smash up my last day and it's none of my business?

(JUDITH moves away from her.)

(Desperately playing for time with a new story.)

This corpse she's pregnant. In the morgue they cut her and out comes this perfect little girl. Dead.

JUDITH: What?

GLORIA: The father's married to a gorgeous Filipina, the dead girl's his white girlfriend. The guy. Works in Sanitation Garage Four, located on a pier in the Hudson River.
This man, he and his wife live in Queens. One night he meets with the girlfriend. Girlfriend's pregnant. She wants the baby to come quick. And the doctor says have sex. Now this guy he never leaves the house at night but this Saturday...

LOUISE: *(Waking.)* Hello pretty lady!

GLORIA: ...he tells his wife, I'm going drinking in Manhattan.

LOUISE: Give me the other shoe.

JUDITH: Why are you still alive?

GLORIA: She calls him but he doesn't pick up...

LOUISE: Why you so mean?

GLORIA: ... because while he's having sex with the girlfriend, he shoots her in the back of the head and dumps her in the Hudson.

JUDITH: Ugh. *(She holds her head.)*

GLORIA: Two a.m. I pick him up with the guys from the precinct. We tell him your girlfriend's dead and he gives this real fake sorrow look. We check his phone. His cell sites were triangulating. So we see that he was at the port exactly where the homicide happened.

JUDITH: You love this!

GLORIA: We find dried blood on the pier where he threw her. He cleaned up but not between the boards. So I'm cuffing him and I'm smiling.

JUDITH: *(Looking at her machine.)* I'm running out of juice here.

GLORIA: He shoots her. And the kid. For a few dollars! To stop having his pay garnished to pay for his child.

GLORIA: And listen to this. It's January. The Hudson's all ice. And two days later, the girlfriend. She floats up. And that's strange because bodies they sink and usually we don't find them 'til spring. Ow! *(Holding her neck.)* My neck.

JUDITH: You saying she floated up deliberately?

Like she's telling you something? Is that what you're saying?

GLORIA: Can a dead body talk?

JUDITH: Stop staring at me!

GLORIA: I've got it!

JUDITH: Got what?

GLORIA: I'm taking you with me.

JUDITH: NO!

GLORIA: You sure dressed for a party.

JUDITH: You. You need to shut up and let me think.

GLORIA: Come on lady!

JUDITH: You want to save me because she floated up. Because of all those dead women. They're inside you. Right?

GLORIA: That girl was fucking someone else's husband. But did she deserve to die?

JUDITH: Yes.

GLORIA: You never did it with a married man?

JUDITH: *(Beat.)* Go to hell!

GLORIA: You any different from her?

JUDITH: Fuck you! *(Beat.)* You, you're sick. Sick from those cadavers you carry. Hell they're even inside you!

GLORIA: And now you, English, you inside me too. But you, you still breathing.

JUDITH: Well you're too late so Mazel Tov and goodbye.

(Switches off and turns.)

GLORIA: *(Yelling.)* Hey lady! Look!

(GLORIA takes out her speech and rips it up.)

JUDITH: *(Turning.)* What are you doing?

GLORIA: Fuck retirement! I'm here! With you! We'll go to my non-retirement party. You and me! Now! Now at least I'm alive!

JUDITH: That's what he said. 'At least I'm alive'.

GLORIA: I'm gonna kick Death in the ass. And you gonna do the same.

JUDITH: Am I?

(A rocked-up version of Schubert's Death and the Maiden comes from LOUISE's ghetto blaster. LOUISE wakes.)

LOUISE: Did she steal my music. The girl? *(To JUDITH.)* You want to dance? Come on! Dance with me! I can be your grandma!

(LOUISE dances. JUDITH pauses before responding by holding out her arms.)

You want to live with me? My daughter! She'll be so mad!

GLORIA: Come on English. Say, what is your name?

JUDITH: OK. Sanchez. You win. But only for a few minutes.

GLORIA: *(Triumphant.)* Yes! Hell, I need a drink and the champagne's getting hot.

(JUDITH moves forward towards her.)

GLORIA: Thank you God. Thank you Jesus.

JUDITH: Hell, I forgot my tape…

(She goes back to get it and takes a few steps towards GLORIA.)

(JUDITH gives a little dance and, as she does, there is the sound from a police siren from the boats below. The arc lights come on and, blinded, she slips and falls into the East River. LOUISE continues dancing. Music is still playing.)

GLORIA: *(Yells.)* She's over. Get the boats! NOW! *(JUDITH's phone is ringing.)*

(Sirens.)

(A woman with the T-shirt "I Heart Brooklyn Bridge" poses for a camera shot. A guy on rollerblades crosses the stage.)

ENDS

Glossary of terms used in *Political Plays*

Yiddish and German words used.

Drek – rubbish. It is commonly used to mean *crap*.

Gatkes – long johns, men's underwear.

Kaez un smetna – cream cheese and sour cream.

Klutz – a clumsy idiot, a fool.

Lobos – a naughty boy, cheeky lad.

Habonim and *Maccabi* – Jewish youth clubs.

Mensch – From the German Das Mensch which means a person. In Yiddish a mensch is a person of great integrity.

Meschugenah – Yiddish (and also German) for crazy.

Nebbish – A misunderstanding of how to pronounce *nebech*. A pathetic person, sad case, saddo.

Schtum – from the German. To keep quiet.

Schlumper – a messily dressed person.

Schmaltz – fat.

Schmuck – prick or dick.

Schwitzing – sweating

Shiksa – A shiksa is Yiddish for a Christian woman. The deeper connotations are that she is usually blonde and the object of desire for a Jewish man. Koby is aware of Susanne's possible use as a honeypot.

Shlang – from Yiddish for snake. Slang for penis. Close to British English dick and like dick is used to mean idiot.

Shlemiel – a fool.

Shlep/schlep – From the German *schleppen*. To drag a heavy weight.

Shlof or *shluf* (depending on your dialect) – sleep.

Shmaltz herring – a fatty herring.

Shtup – from Yiddish, to shove. Slang close to British English to shag.

Schwitzing – Sweating.

Yiddish Lullaby.

Shlof, Mayn Kind

(English translation by Julia Pascal)

> Shlof mayn kind, mayn kroyn, mayn sheyner,
> Shlofzhe, zunenyu.
> Shlof, mayn lebn, mayn kaddish eyner,
> Lulinke lu-lu.
>
> Sleep my child, my crown, my beauty,
>
> Sleep, my darling son.
> Sleep, my life, my only Kaddish,
> Lulinke lu-lu.

Hebrew

Shalom chaver – hello friend.

L'chaim – The traditional toast when drinking. It means to life!

Ayze Balagan – What a mess!

OTHER JULIA PASCAL TITLES

The Shylock Play
9781840028126

Pascal: Crossing Jerusalem and Other Plays
Includes the plays Crossing Jerusalem, The Golem, Year Zero and St Joan
9781840023619

Pascal: The Holocaust Trilogy
Includes the plays Theresa, A Dead Woman on Holiday and The Dybbuk
9781840020946

The Yiddish Queen Yiddish Lear / Woman in the Moon
9781840022537

WWW.OBERONBOOKS.COM

Follow us on www.twitter.com/@oberonbooks
& www.facebook.com/oberonbook